Somatic Detox Diet: A Comprehensive Guide

Written by: Charlotte Emily

Copyright © 2024

All Rights Reserved.

No part of this publication or the information contained herein may be reproduced or quoted in any form including printing, scanning, or photocopying without the prior written permission of the copyright holder.

Disclaimer and Terms of Use: Every effort has been made to ensure the accuracy and completeness of the information in this book. However, the author and publisher cannot guarantee its accuracy due to the rapidly evolving nature of science, research, and internet information. The author and publisher disclaim any responsibility for errors, omissions, or misinterpretation of the subject matter. This book is provided for informational and motivational purposes only. Always consult a licensed professional before making any lifestyle or dietary changes.

Table of Contents

Table of Contents.. 3

Introduction...4

    Overview of the topic... 4

Chapter 1: Understanding Detox Diets........................9

    Definition and History of Detox Diets.......................9

    Common Principles and Practices........................... 11

    Benefits and Criticisms of Detox Diets................... 14

Chapter 2: The Concept of Somatic Detox................20

    Definition of Somatic Detox...................................20

    Differences Between Somatic Detox and Traditional Detox Diets.. 21

    Scientific Basis and Emerging Research................ 26

Chapter 3: Principles of the Somatic Detox Diet...... 33

    Core Principles and Guidelines.............................. 33

The Role of Whole Foods and Natural Ingredients. 37

Importance of Hydration and Specific Fluids 40

Mind-Body Connection and Its Role in Detoxification 43

Chapter 4: Foods to Include in the Somatic Detox Diet 49

Fruits and Vegetables 49

Whole Grains and Legumes 54

Nuts and Seeds 58

Herbs and Spices 62

Examples of Specific Detoxifying Foods 65

Chapter 5: Foods to Avoid 69

Processed Foods and Refined Sugars 69

Caffeine and Alcohol 73

Artificial Additives and Preservatives 77

Common Allergens and Irritants............................80

Chapter 6: Meal Planning and Recipes..................... 85

Weekly Meal Planning Strategies........................... 85

Sample Meal Plans for Different Dietary Preferences. 89

Breakfast, Lunch, Dinner, and Snack Recipes.........93

Tips for Preparing and Storing Meals.................... 109

Chapter 7: The Role of Supplements and Herbal Remedies... 114

Overview of Beneficial Supplements..................... 114

Herbal Remedies and Their Detoxifying Properties.... 118

How to Safely Incorporate Supplements into the Diet 123

Precautions and Contraindications....................... 126

Chapter 8: Hydration and Detoxification................133

Importance of Water in the Detox Process............ 133

Recommended Daily Water Intake........................ 136

Detoxifying Beverages.. 139

Recipes for Detox Drinks....................................... 143

Chapter 9: Physical Activity and Somatic Detox....150

The Role of Exercise in Detoxification.................. 150

Creating a Balanced Routine.................................. 161

Chapter 10: Monitoring Progress and Adjusting the Diet.. 167

Tracking Physical and Mental Changes.................167

Recognizing Signs of Effective Detoxification..... 172

Adjusting the Diet Based on Individual Needs......174

Seeking Professional Guidance.............................. 178

Chapter 11: Case Studies and Personal Experiences... 184

Testimonials from Individuals Who Have Tried the Somatic Detox Diet..................................184

Analysis of Their Experiences and Results........... 188

Chapter 12: Debunking Common Myths About Detox Diets..199

Addressing Misconceptions and Misinformation..199

Clarifying Common Myths About Detox Diets.....210

Chapter 13: Comparing the Somatic Detox Diet to Other Detox Methods... 215

Nutritional Differences and Similarities................ 215

Health Impacts Comparison................................. 222

Consumer Preferences and Perceptions.................227

Chapter 14: Expert Opinions and Research Findings. 233

Compilation of Expert Viewpoints........................ 233

Summary of Recent Research Findings.................236

Future Directions for Research on the Somatic Detox Diet... 240

Conclusion.. **246**

Introduction

Overview of the topic

In recent years, the concept of detox diets has gained immense popularity as individuals seek ways to cleanse their bodies of toxins and improve their overall health. Among the various detox methods, the Somatic Detox Diet stands out for its holistic approach, which integrates the principles of whole foods, hydration, and the mind-body connection. This comprehensive guide aims to explore the Somatic Detox Diet in detail, providing readers with valuable insights into its principles, benefits, and practical applications.

Importance of understanding the Somatic Detox Diet

Understanding the Somatic Detox Diet is crucial for anyone looking to adopt a healthier lifestyle and improve their well-being. Unlike traditional detox diets that often focus solely on eliminating toxins, the Somatic Detox Diet emphasizes a balanced approach that supports the body's natural detoxification processes while nourishing the mind and body. By gaining a thorough understanding of this diet, individuals can make informed decisions and achieve lasting health benefits.

Purpose and goals of the article

The primary purpose of this article is to provide a comprehensive and balanced examination of the Somatic Detox Diet. This will be achieved by presenting detailed information on its principles, foods to include and avoid, meal planning, and the role of physical activity and supplements. The article aims to offer readers a thorough understanding of both the positive and negative aspects of the Somatic Detox Diet, enabling them to make informed dietary choices.

The goals of the article are as follows:

1. Inform and Educate: To provide readers with accurate and up-to-date information on the principles and health effects of the Somatic Detox Diet. This includes an in-depth analysis of

foods, supplements, hydration, and physical activity.

2. Present Scientific Evidence: To review and synthesize findings from various scientific studies on the Somatic Detox Diet, highlighting both the potential risks and benefits.

3. Debunk Myths and Misconceptions: To address common myths and misconceptions about detox diets, separating fact from fiction based on scientific evidence.

4. Compare with Other Detox Methods: To compare the Somatic Detox Diet with other popular detox methods, providing a clear understanding of the differences in their nutritional content and potential health effects.

5. Offer Practical Tips and Recommendations: To suggest practical tips for adopting the Somatic Detox Diet, including meal planning, recipes, and strategies for incorporating physical activity and supplements.

6. Encourage Critical Thinking: To encourage readers to critically evaluate their dietary choices and consider the long-term implications of their detox practices. By fostering a better understanding of the Somatic Detox Diet and its potential effects, the article aims to empower readers to make healthier decisions.

This article will serve as a comprehensive guide for anyone seeking to understand the potential health impacts of the Somatic Detox Diet. By presenting a balanced view based on scientific research, expert opinions, and personal experiences, it will provide readers with the knowledge and tools needed to make informed dietary choices. Whether you are new to detox diets or looking to deepen your understanding of the Somatic Detox Diet, this article aims to offer valuable insights into one of the most holistic approaches to detoxification.

Chapter 1: Understanding Detox Diets

Definition and History of Detox Diets

Detox diets, often referred to as detoxification diets, are nutritional strategies designed to remove toxins from the body. These diets typically involve a period of fasting followed by a strict regimen of fruits, vegetables, juices, and water. The underlying principle is to cleanse the body of harmful substances accumulated from environmental pollutants, processed foods, and other external sources. Detox diets claim to enhance the body's natural detoxification processes, improve health, and promote weight loss.

History

The concept of detoxification is not new. It dates back to ancient civilizations, where detox practices were integral to various healing traditions. In ancient Egypt, Greece, and Rome, detoxification was achieved through methods such as fasting, enemas, and the use of herbs. Traditional Chinese Medicine (TCM) and Ayurveda, two of the oldest medical systems, also emphasize the importance of detoxification. TCM promotes practices like acupuncture, herbal medicine, and dietary modifications to remove toxins and restore balance, while Ayurveda advocates for Panchakarma, a five-step detox program involving massage, herbal therapy, and dietary changes.

In the modern era, the popularity of detox diets surged in the late 20th century, largely influenced by the wellness movement and the growing awareness of environmental toxins. Celebrities and health gurus have played a significant role in promoting various detox diets, contributing to their mainstream acceptance.

Common Principles and Practices

Principles

Detox diets vary widely, but they share several common principles:

1. **Elimination of Toxins:** The primary goal is to eliminate substances considered harmful to the body. This includes processed foods, sugar, caffeine, alcohol, and certain fats.

2. **Nutrient-Rich Intake:** These diets emphasize the consumption of nutrient-dense foods, primarily organic fruits and vegetables, to provide essential vitamins, minerals, and antioxidants.

3. **Hydration:** Adequate water intake is crucial to support kidney function and facilitate the elimination of toxins through urine.

4. **Digestive Rest:** Detox diets often include periods of fasting or consuming easily digestible foods to give the digestive system a break and allow the body to focus on detoxification.

5. **Supportive Supplements:** Some detox programs incorporate supplements like probiotics, fiber, and herbs known for their detoxifying properties.

Practices

1. **Juice Cleanses:** Juice cleanses involve consuming only fresh fruit and vegetable juices for a specified period. These cleanses are believed to flood the body with nutrients while allowing the digestive system to rest.

2. **Fasting:** Intermittent fasting or complete fasting for short periods is a common practice in detox diets. Fasting is thought to trigger autophagy, a process where the body cleans out damaged cells and regenerates new ones.

3. **Elimination Diets:** These diets remove potential allergens and irritants, such as gluten, dairy, and soy, to reduce inflammation and improve gut health.

4. **Herbal Teas and Supplements:** Herbal teas like dandelion root and milk thistle are often consumed to support liver function, while supplements like activated charcoal are used to bind toxins in the gut.

5. **Hydrotherapy:** Techniques such as colonics and enemas are used to cleanse the colon, although these practices are controversial and not universally recommended.

Benefits and Criticisms of Detox Diets

Benefits

1. **Increased Nutrient Intake:** Detox diets emphasize the consumption of fresh fruits and vegetables, which can boost the intake of essential nutrients and antioxidants, potentially improving overall health.

2. **Improved Digestion:** Eliminating processed foods and potential allergens can alleviate digestive issues such as bloating, gas, and indigestion. Some people report enhanced gut health and regularity.

3. **Weight Loss:** Many detox diets result in short-term weight loss due to reduced calorie

intake and the elimination of high-calorie, low-nutrient foods.

4. **Enhanced Energy Levels:** Proponents of detox diets often report increased energy levels and improved mental clarity, which may result from reduced consumption of caffeine and sugar.

5. **Better Skin Health:** Some individuals experience clearer skin and reduced acne, possibly due to the elimination of dietary triggers and increased hydration.

6. **Mental and Emotional Benefits:** The discipline required for a detox diet can foster a sense of accomplishment and mindfulness, contributing to improved mental and emotional well-being.

Criticisms

1. **Lack of Scientific Evidence:** Critics argue that there is limited scientific evidence to support the efficacy of detox diets. The body is equipped with natural detoxification systems, including the

liver, kidneys, and lungs, which can effectively eliminate toxins without the need for extreme dietary interventions.

2. **Nutrient Deficiencies:** Strict detox diets, especially those involving prolonged fasting or juice cleanses, can lead to nutrient deficiencies. Essential macronutrients like protein and fats may be lacking, which can adversely affect muscle mass, metabolism, and overall health.

3. **Short-Term Solutions:** While detox diets may offer quick results, they are often not sustainable long-term solutions. Many individuals regain the weight lost during a detox once they return to their regular eating habits.

4. **Potential for Disordered Eating:** The restrictive nature of detox diets can promote unhealthy relationships with food and may contribute to disordered eating patterns. The emphasis on "clean" and "toxic" foods can lead to obsessive behaviors and anxiety around eating.

5. **Dehydration and Electrolyte Imbalance:** Some detox practices, particularly those involving colonics and enemas, can lead to dehydration and electrolyte imbalances, posing serious health risks.

6. **Misleading Marketing:** Detox diets are often marketed with exaggerated claims and testimonials that lack scientific validation. Consumers may be misled into believing that detox diets can cure diseases or provide miraculous health benefits.

Detox diets, with their historical roots and modern popularity, offer a variety of approaches to cleansing the body and improving health. While they can provide benefits such as increased nutrient intake, improved digestion, and short-term weight loss, they are also subject to significant criticisms. The lack of scientific evidence, potential for nutrient deficiencies, and risk of promoting disordered eating are important considerations.

For individuals interested in detox diets, it is crucial to approach them with a balanced perspective and to consult with healthcare professionals before making significant dietary changes. A sustainable approach to health should prioritize a balanced, nutrient-rich diet and lifestyle habits that support the body's natural detoxification processes. By understanding both the benefits and limitations of detox diets, individuals can make informed choices that align with their health goals and overall well-being.

Chapter 2: The Concept of Somatic Detox

Definition of Somatic Detox

Somatic Detox refers to a holistic approach to detoxification that not only focuses on cleansing the body of physical toxins but also addresses the mind-body connection. The term "somatic" derives from the Greek word "soma," meaning "body," and in this context, it emphasizes the integration of physical and psychological health. Somatic Detox aims to enhance overall well-being by combining dietary practices, physical activities, and mental health strategies to support the body's natural detoxification processes and improve emotional and psychological health.

The core philosophy of Somatic Detox is that the body and mind are interconnected, and both need to be nurtured and cleansed for optimal health. This approach recognizes that stress, negative emotions, and mental clutter can contribute to physical ailments and impede the body's ability to detoxify efficiently. Therefore, Somatic Detox incorporates elements such as mindfulness, stress management, and emotional healing alongside traditional dietary detox practices.

Differences Between Somatic Detox and Traditional Detox Diets

Holistic Approach vs. Focused Approach

Traditional detox diets typically emphasize dietary changes to eliminate toxins from the body. These diets may involve fasting, juice cleanses, or the elimination of specific foods believed to be harmful. While these methods can be effective in promoting physical detoxification, they often overlook the psychological and emotional aspects of well-being.

In contrast, Somatic Detox adopts a holistic approach, integrating physical, mental, and emotional health. This comprehensive strategy acknowledges that the mind and body are interconnected and that mental and emotional health play a crucial role in the body's ability to detoxify. Somatic Detox includes practices such as meditation, yoga, and other mind-body therapies to support emotional balance and reduce stress, which can enhance the effectiveness of physical detoxification.

Dietary Practices

Traditional detox diets often have a strict focus on dietary restrictions, such as eliminating processed foods, sugars, caffeine, and alcohol. These diets may involve consuming only specific foods or beverages, like green juices or detox teas, for a set period. The primary goal is to cleanse the digestive system and reduce the intake of toxins.

Somatic Detox, while also emphasizing clean and nutrient-dense foods, places a greater emphasis on the quality of food and its impact on overall well-being. The diet in a Somatic Detox program includes a variety of whole foods, such as organic fruits and vegetables, whole grains, lean proteins, and healthy fats, ensuring that the body receives essential nutrients. Additionally,

Somatic Detox encourages mindful eating practices, where individuals are more aware of their food choices, eating habits, and the sensations of hunger and satiety.

Physical Activity and Movement

Traditional detox diets may include recommendations for physical activity, but they often do not emphasize the importance of movement in the detoxification process. Exercise is seen as a supplementary activity rather than a core component.

Somatic Detox, however, integrates physical activity as a fundamental aspect of the detox process. It encourages practices such as yoga, tai chi, and other forms of gentle exercise that promote circulation, support lymphatic drainage, and enhance the body's natural detoxification pathways. These activities not only help in physical cleansing but also contribute to mental clarity and emotional balance.

Mind-Body Connection

One of the most significant differences between Somatic Detox and traditional detox diets is the emphasis on the mind-body connection. Traditional detox diets focus primarily on physical health, often neglecting the psychological and emotional components.

Somatic Detox recognizes the importance of mental and emotional health in overall well-being. It incorporates practices such as meditation, mindfulness, and breathwork to help individuals manage stress, release emotional toxins, and cultivate a sense of inner peace. By addressing the mental and emotional aspects of health, Somatic Detox aims to create a more comprehensive and lasting impact on overall wellness.

Scientific Basis and Emerging Research

Detoxification Pathways

The human body has several natural detoxification pathways, including the liver, kidneys, lungs, skin, and digestive system. These organs work together to eliminate toxins and maintain homeostasis. The liver, for example, plays a crucial role in metabolizing and excreting various substances, while the kidneys filter waste products from the blood. The skin can excrete toxins through sweat, and the lungs expel carbon dioxide and other gaseous wastes.

Research supports the effectiveness of certain dietary and lifestyle practices in enhancing these detoxification pathways. For example, studies have shown that consuming a diet rich in fruits, vegetables, and fiber can support liver function and promote the elimination of toxins through the digestive system. Hydration is also critical, as water is essential for kidney function and helps flush toxins from the body.

Role of Nutrition

Emerging research highlights the role of specific nutrients and foods in supporting detoxification. Antioxidants, found in fruits and vegetables, help neutralize free radicals and reduce oxidative stress, which can damage cells and contribute to chronic diseases. Cruciferous vegetables, such as broccoli, kale, and Brussels sprouts, contain compounds that enhance the liver's detoxification enzymes.

Probiotics and prebiotics, which support gut health, are also gaining attention for their role in detoxification. A healthy gut microbiome can improve digestion, enhance nutrient absorption, and support the immune system. Research suggests that a balanced gut microbiome can influence the body's ability to detoxify and protect against harmful substances.

Physical Activity and Detoxification

Physical activity is known to have numerous health benefits, including supporting detoxification. Exercise promotes circulation and lymphatic drainage, which are essential for the removal of toxins from tissues and the transportation of waste products to excretory organs. Sweating during exercise can also help eliminate toxins through the skin.

Studies have shown that regular physical activity can reduce inflammation, improve immune function, and enhance overall metabolic health. Practices such as yoga and tai chi, which are integral to Somatic Detox, have been found to reduce stress, improve mental health, and support physical detoxification.

Mind-Body Practices

The scientific basis for the mind-body connection is well-established, with research demonstrating the impact of mental and emotional health on physical well-being. Chronic stress, for example, can impair immune function, increase inflammation, and disrupt the body's natural detoxification processes.

Mind-body practices, such as meditation and mindfulness, have been shown to reduce stress, improve mental clarity, and enhance emotional resilience. These practices can modulate the stress response by lowering cortisol levels, which can support immune function and overall health.

Emerging Research

Recent studies have explored the benefits of integrative approaches to detoxification, such as Somatic Detox. For example, research on mindfulness-based stress reduction (MBSR) has shown that mindfulness practices can improve emotional well-being, reduce stress, and enhance immune function. Studies on yoga and tai chi have demonstrated their positive effects on mental health, physical fitness, and overall quality of life.

Additionally, research on the gut-brain axis highlights the bidirectional communication between the gut and the brain, emphasizing the importance of gut health in mental and emotional well-being. This emerging field supports the integration of dietary practices, gut health, and mind-body therapies in a comprehensive detox program.

Somatic Detox represents a holistic and integrative approach to detoxification that addresses both physical and psychological health. By recognizing the interconnectedness of the body and mind, Somatic Detox offers a comprehensive strategy for enhancing overall well-being. This approach differs from traditional detox diets by emphasizing the importance of mental and emotional health, incorporating physical activity, and promoting mindful eating practices.

The scientific basis for Somatic Detox is supported by research on the body's natural detoxification pathways, the role of nutrition, the benefits of physical activity, and the impact of mind-body practices. Emerging research continues to explore the benefits of integrative approaches to health and detoxification, highlighting the potential of Somatic Detox to support long-term wellness.

As the understanding of the mind-body connection and holistic health continues to evolve, Somatic Detox offers a promising framework for individuals seeking a balanced and sustainable approach to detoxification. By integrating dietary practices, physical activity, and mental health strategies, Somatic Detox aims to create a more comprehensive and lasting impact on overall health and well-being.

Chapter 3: Principles of the Somatic Detox Diet

Core Principles and Guidelines

The Somatic Detox Diet is rooted in the understanding that optimal health and detoxification require a holistic approach that integrates dietary practices, hydration, physical activity, and mental well-being. The core principles and guidelines of the Somatic Detox Diet focus on promoting natural detoxification processes, supporting overall health, and enhancing the mind-body connection.

Principle 1: Emphasis on Whole Foods

The foundation of the Somatic Detox Diet is the consumption of whole, unprocessed foods. These foods are rich in essential nutrients, including vitamins, minerals, antioxidants, and fiber, which support the body's natural detoxification pathways. Whole foods include fresh fruits and vegetables, whole grains, legumes, nuts, seeds, and lean proteins. By prioritizing these nutrient-dense foods, the Somatic Detox Diet aims to reduce the intake of toxins and provide the body with the building blocks needed for optimal health.

Principle 2: Hydration

Adequate hydration is crucial for detoxification. Water is essential for the proper functioning of the kidneys, liver, and digestive system, which are key organs involved in detoxification. The Somatic Detox Diet emphasizes the importance of drinking plenty of water throughout the day to support the elimination of toxins through urine and sweat. Additionally, specific fluids such as herbal teas and infused waters are recommended for their detoxifying properties.

Principle 3: Mindful Eating

Mindful eating is a core component of the Somatic Detox Diet. This practice involves paying attention to the body's hunger and satiety signals, eating slowly, and savoring each bite. Mindful eating encourages individuals to be present during meals, which can improve digestion, prevent overeating, and enhance the overall eating experience. It also fosters a deeper connection between the mind and body, which is essential for holistic health.

Principle 4: Physical Activity

Physical activity is integral to the Somatic Detox Diet. Regular exercise promotes circulation, supports lymphatic drainage, and enhances the body's natural detoxification processes. The diet encourages a variety of physical activities, including cardiovascular exercise, strength training, yoga, and tai chi. These activities not only support physical detoxification but also contribute to mental clarity and emotional balance.

Principle 5: Stress Management and Emotional Health

Recognizing the impact of stress and emotional health on overall well-being, the Somatic Detox Diet incorporates practices such as meditation, mindfulness, and breathwork. These techniques help manage stress, reduce anxiety, and promote emotional resilience. By addressing the psychological aspects of health, the diet aims to create a balanced and harmonious mind-body connection, which is crucial for effective detoxification.

The Role of Whole Foods and Natural Ingredients

Nutrient Density and Detoxification

Whole foods are the cornerstone of the Somatic Detox Diet because of their high nutrient density. These foods provide essential vitamins, minerals, and antioxidants that support the body's detoxification processes. For example, vitamins A, C, and E are powerful antioxidants that help neutralize free radicals and reduce oxidative stress. Minerals such as zinc, selenium, and magnesium play critical roles in enzymatic reactions involved in detoxification.

Fiber and Digestive Health

Dietary fiber, found in fruits, vegetables, whole grains, and legumes, is crucial for digestive health and detoxification. Fiber supports regular bowel movements, which helps eliminate waste products and toxins from the body. Soluble fiber, in particular, can bind to toxins in the digestive tract and facilitate their removal. Additionally, a high-fiber diet supports a healthy gut microbiome, which is essential for overall health and effective detoxification.

Phytochemicals and Antioxidants

Phytochemicals are naturally occurring compounds in plants that have been shown to have numerous health benefits, including detoxification. These compounds, such as flavonoids, carotenoids, and polyphenols, have antioxidant and anti-inflammatory properties. They support the liver's detoxification enzymes, enhance the body's ability to eliminate toxins, and protect cells from damage. Consuming a variety of colorful fruits and vegetables ensures a diverse intake of these beneficial phytochemicals.

Natural Ingredients for Detoxification

Certain natural ingredients are particularly effective in supporting detoxification. For example, cruciferous vegetables such as broccoli, kale, and Brussels sprouts contain sulfur-containing compounds that enhance the liver's detoxification enzymes. Garlic and onions are rich in sulfur compounds that support the production of glutathione, a key antioxidant involved in detoxification. Herbs such as cilantro and parsley can help chelate heavy metals and facilitate their removal from the body.

Importance of Hydration and Specific Fluids

Water and Detoxification

Water is essential for every bodily function, including detoxification. It supports the kidneys in filtering waste products from the blood and excreting them through urine. Adequate hydration also supports bowel movements, preventing constipation and promoting the elimination of toxins through the digestive system. The

Somatic Detox Diet recommends drinking at least eight 8-ounce glasses of water per day, with adjustments based on individual needs and activity levels.

Herbal Teas

Herbal teas are an excellent addition to the Somatic Detox Diet because of their detoxifying properties. For example, dandelion root tea supports liver function and stimulates bile production, which aids in the digestion and elimination of fats and toxins. Milk thistle tea contains silymarin, a compound known for its liver-protective effects. Green tea is rich in catechins, antioxidants that enhance liver function and support the elimination of toxins.

Infused Waters

Infused waters are a flavorful way to stay hydrated and support detoxification. These beverages are made by adding fruits, vegetables, and herbs to water, which infuse the water with beneficial compounds. For example, lemon water is rich in vitamin C, an antioxidant that supports liver function and boosts the immune system. Cucumber water is hydrating and has anti-inflammatory properties, while mint water can aid digestion and provide a refreshing taste.

Electrolytes

Electrolytes, such as sodium, potassium, and magnesium, are essential for maintaining fluid balance and supporting the body's detoxification processes. The Somatic Detox Diet encourages the consumption of natural sources of electrolytes, such as coconut water, which is rich in potassium and other minerals. This helps ensure proper hydration and supports the body's ability to detoxify effectively.

Mind-Body Connection and Its Role in Detoxification

Stress and Detoxification

Chronic stress can negatively impact the body's detoxification processes. High levels of stress hormones, such as cortisol, can impair liver function, increase inflammation, and disrupt the balance of the gut microbiome. The Somatic Detox Diet emphasizes stress management techniques, such as meditation, mindfulness, and breathwork, to reduce stress and support the body's natural detoxification pathways.

Mindfulness and Eating Practices

Mindful eating is a practice that involves paying full attention to the eating experience, including the taste, texture, and aroma of food, as well as the body's hunger and satiety signals. This practice can improve digestion, prevent overeating, and enhance the overall enjoyment of food. By fostering a deeper connection between the mind and body, mindful eating supports the holistic approach of the Somatic Detox Diet and promotes better health outcomes.

Meditation and Emotional Health

Meditation is a powerful tool for enhancing mental and emotional well-being. Regular meditation practice has been shown to reduce stress, improve mood, and increase emotional resilience. By promoting relaxation and reducing anxiety, meditation can help support the body's detoxification processes. The Somatic Detox Diet encourages incorporating meditation into daily routines to create a balanced and harmonious mind-body connection.

Yoga and Physical Detoxification

Yoga is an integral part of the Somatic Detox Diet because of its dual benefits for physical and mental health. Yoga poses and sequences promote circulation, support lymphatic drainage, and enhance the function of detoxification organs such as the liver and kidneys. Additionally, the mindful and meditative aspects of yoga help reduce stress and improve mental clarity. Practicing yoga regularly can support overall detoxification and enhance well-being.

Breathwork and Detoxification

Breathwork, or controlled breathing exercises, can have a profound impact on the body's detoxification processes. Deep breathing techniques increase oxygen intake, improve lung function, and enhance the elimination of carbon dioxide and other waste products. Breathwork also activates the parasympathetic nervous system, promoting relaxation and reducing stress. The Somatic Detox Diet incorporates breathwork practices to support both physical and emotional detoxification.

The principles of the Somatic Detox Diet encompass a holistic and integrative approach to detoxification, emphasizing the importance of whole foods, hydration, physical activity, and the mind-body connection. By focusing on nutrient-dense whole foods and natural ingredients, the diet provides essential nutrients that support the body's natural detoxification processes. Adequate hydration, including the consumption of herbal teas and infused waters, is crucial for effective detoxification.

Mindful eating practices, stress management techniques, and the integration of physical activities such as yoga and breathwork further enhance the body's ability to detoxify and promote overall well-being. The Somatic Detox Diet recognizes the interconnectedness of physical, mental, and emotional health, offering a comprehensive strategy for achieving optimal health and long-term wellness.

By adhering to these core principles and guidelines, individuals can support their body's natural detoxification processes, reduce the intake of toxins, and foster a balanced and harmonious mind-body connection. The Somatic Detox Diet provides a sustainable and effective approach to detoxification, promoting health and well-being in a holistic and integrative manner.

Chapter 4: Foods to Include in the Somatic Detox Diet

Fruits and Vegetables

Fruits and vegetables form the cornerstone of the Somatic Detox Diet due to their high nutrient density, fiber content, and antioxidant properties. These foods provide essential vitamins, minerals, and phytochemicals that support the body's detoxification processes, enhance immune function, and promote overall health.

Fruits

Fruits are rich in vitamins, antioxidants, and fiber, making them an essential component of the Somatic Detox Diet. They provide natural sweetness and a wide range of health benefits:

- **Berries**: Blueberries, strawberries, raspberries, and blackberries are packed with antioxidants, particularly vitamin C and anthocyanins. These compounds help neutralize free radicals, reduce inflammation, and support liver detoxification. Berries are also high in fiber, which aids in digestion and helps remove toxins from the digestive tract.

- **Citrus Fruits**: Oranges, lemons, limes, and grapefruits are excellent sources of vitamin C, a powerful antioxidant that supports the immune system and enhances the liver's detoxification enzymes. Citrus fruits also stimulate bile production, aiding in the digestion and elimination of fats and toxins.

- **Apples**: Apples contain pectin, a type of soluble fiber that binds to toxins in the digestive tract and helps eliminate them from the body. They also provide antioxidants like quercetin, which supports liver health and reduces inflammation.

- **Avocados**: Avocados are rich in healthy monounsaturated fats, which support heart health and provide essential nutrients for detoxification.

They also contain glutathione, a potent antioxidant that aids in liver detoxification.

- **Pineapple**: Pineapple is a good source of bromelain, an enzyme that aids in digestion and has anti-inflammatory properties. It also provides vitamin C and manganese, both of which support overall health and detoxification.

Vegetables

Vegetables are nutrient-dense and low in calories, making them ideal for a detox diet. They provide essential vitamins, minerals, and fiber, and many have specific detoxifying properties:

- **Cruciferous Vegetables**: Broccoli, cauliflower, Brussels sprouts, kale, and cabbage are rich in sulfur-containing compounds like glucosinolates. These compounds enhance the liver's detoxification enzymes and support the elimination of toxins. Cruciferous vegetables are also high in fiber and antioxidants, promoting overall health.

- **Leafy Greens**: Spinach, Swiss chard, arugula, and collard greens are excellent sources of chlorophyll, which helps remove toxins from the blood and supports liver function. Leafy greens are also rich in vitamins A, C, and K, as well as folate and iron.

- **Root Vegetables**: Carrots, beets, and sweet potatoes are high in antioxidants, vitamins, and fiber. Beets, in particular, contain betaine and pectin, which support liver detoxification and bile production. Carrots provide beta-carotene, which converts to vitamin A and supports immune function.

- **Allium Vegetables**: Garlic, onions, leeks, and shallots contain sulfur compounds that enhance the liver's detoxification pathways. Garlic, for example, boosts the production of glutathione and has antimicrobial properties that support immune health.

- **Bell Peppers**: Bell peppers are rich in vitamin C, antioxidants, and fiber. They support immune function, reduce inflammation, and enhance the body's detoxification processes.

Whole Grains and Legumes

Whole grains and legumes are important sources of complex carbohydrates, fiber, protein, and essential nutrients. They provide sustained energy, support digestive health, and help eliminate toxins from the body.

Whole Grains

Whole grains retain all parts of the grain kernel, including the bran, germ, and endosperm, which provides a rich source of nutrients and fiber:

- **Quinoa**: Quinoa is a complete protein, meaning it contains all nine essential amino acids. It is also high in fiber, magnesium, and antioxidants, making it an excellent choice for a detox diet.

- **Brown Rice**: Brown rice is a whole grain that provides fiber, B vitamins, and minerals like magnesium and selenium. It supports digestive health and helps stabilize blood sugar levels.

- **Oats**: Oats are rich in soluble fiber, particularly beta-glucan, which helps lower cholesterol levels and supports heart health. They also provide antioxidants and essential nutrients like manganese and phosphorus.

- **Barley**: Barley is high in fiber, which promotes digestive health and helps regulate blood sugar levels. It also provides vitamins and minerals such as selenium, magnesium, and B vitamins.

- **Millet**: Millet is a gluten-free grain that provides fiber, protein, and antioxidants. It supports digestive health and helps maintain steady energy levels.

Legumes

Legumes are a diverse group of plant foods that include beans, lentils, and peas. They are rich in protein, fiber, vitamins, and minerals:

- **Lentils**: Lentils are high in protein, fiber, and essential nutrients such as folate, iron, and manganese. They support digestive health, stabilize blood sugar levels, and provide sustained energy.

- **Chickpeas**: Chickpeas, also known as garbanzo beans, are rich in protein, fiber, and antioxidants. They support digestive health, reduce inflammation, and provide essential nutrients like folate and magnesium.

- **Black Beans**: Black beans are high in protein, fiber, and antioxidants, particularly anthocyanins. They support heart health, regulate blood sugar levels, and promote digestive health.

- **Kidney Beans**: Kidney beans are rich in protein, fiber, and essential nutrients such as folate, iron, and potassium. They support overall health and provide sustained energy.

- **Green Peas**: Green peas are a good source of protein, fiber, vitamins, and minerals. They support digestive health, reduce inflammation, and provide antioxidants.

Nuts and Seeds

Nuts and seeds are nutrient-dense foods that provide healthy fats, protein, fiber, vitamins, and minerals. They support heart health, provide sustained energy, and enhance the body's detoxification processes.

Nuts

- **Almonds**: Almonds are rich in healthy monounsaturated fats, protein, fiber, and essential nutrients such as vitamin E, magnesium, and calcium. They support heart health, provide sustained energy, and promote digestive health.

- **Walnuts**: Walnuts are high in omega-3 fatty acids, antioxidants, and essential nutrients such as manganese and copper. They support brain health, reduce inflammation, and provide sustained energy.

- **Cashews**: Cashews provide healthy fats, protein, and essential nutrients such as magnesium, phosphorus, and zinc. They support bone health, provide sustained energy, and promote overall health.

- **Pistachios**: Pistachios are rich in healthy fats, protein, fiber, and antioxidants. They support heart health, regulate blood sugar levels, and provide sustained energy.

- **Brazil Nuts**: Brazil nuts are an excellent source of selenium, a mineral that supports thyroid function and enhances the body's detoxification processes. They also provide healthy fats and protein.

Seeds

- **Chia Seeds**: Chia seeds are rich in omega-3 fatty acids, fiber, protein, and antioxidants. They support digestive health, reduce inflammation, and provide sustained energy.

- **Flaxseeds**: Flaxseeds are high in omega-3 fatty acids, fiber, and lignans, which have antioxidant properties. They support heart health, promote digestive health, and reduce inflammation.

- **Pumpkin Seeds**: Pumpkin seeds are a good source of protein, healthy fats, fiber, and essential nutrients such as magnesium, zinc, and iron. They support immune function, reduce inflammation, and provide sustained energy.

- **Sunflower Seeds**: Sunflower seeds are rich in healthy fats, protein, fiber, and antioxidants such as vitamin E. They support heart health, reduce inflammation, and provide sustained energy.

- **Sesame Seeds**: Sesame seeds provide healthy fats, protein, and essential nutrients such as calcium, magnesium, and zinc. They support bone health, reduce inflammation, and promote overall health.

Herbs and Spices

Herbs and spices are not only flavorful additions to meals but also provide numerous health benefits, including supporting detoxification processes, reducing inflammation, and enhancing immune function.

Herbs

- **Cilantro**: Cilantro is known for its ability to bind to heavy metals and facilitate their removal from the body. It also has antioxidant and anti-inflammatory properties.

- **Parsley**: Parsley is rich in vitamins A, C, and K, as well as antioxidants such as flavonoids. It supports kidney function, reduces inflammation, and enhances overall detoxification.

- **Basil**: Basil contains essential oils with anti-inflammatory and antimicrobial properties. It supports liver function, reduces inflammation, and enhances overall health.

- **Mint**: Mint has digestive benefits and can help relieve indigestion and bloating. It also has antioxidant properties and supports overall detoxification.

- **Rosemary**: Rosemary is rich in antioxidants such as rosmarinic acid and carnosic acid. It supports liver function, reduces inflammation, and enhances overall health.

Spices

- **Turmeric**: Turmeric contains curcumin, a powerful anti-inflammatory and antioxidant compound. It supports liver function, reduces inflammation, and enhances overall detoxification.

- **Ginger**: Ginger has anti-inflammatory and digestive benefits. It supports digestion, reduces inflammation, and enhances overall detoxification.

- **Cinnamon**: Cinnamon is rich in antioxidants and has anti-inflammatory properties. It supports blood sugar regulation, reduces inflammation, and enhances overall health.

- **Garlic**: Garlic contains sulfur compounds that support liver detoxification and enhance the immune system. It has antimicrobial and anti-inflammatory properties.

- **Cayenne Pepper**: Cayenne pepper contains capsaicin, which has antioxidant and anti-inflammatory properties. It supports digestion, enhances metabolism, and promotes overall detoxification.

Examples of Specific Detoxifying Foods

Certain foods are particularly effective in supporting the body's detoxification processes due to their unique properties and nutrient profiles:

- **Lemons**: Lemons are rich in vitamin C, which supports liver function and boosts the immune system. They also stimulate bile production, aiding in the digestion and elimination of fats and toxins.

- **Beets**: Beets contain betaine and pectin, which support liver detoxification and bile production. They are also high in antioxidants and fiber, promoting overall health.

- **Garlic**: Garlic boosts the production of glutathione, a key antioxidant involved in liver detoxification. It also has antimicrobial properties that support immune health.

- **Green Tea**: Green tea is rich in catechins, antioxidants that enhance liver function and support the elimination of toxins. It also has anti-inflammatory properties.

- **Dandelion Greens**: Dandelion greens support liver function and stimulate bile production. They are also rich in vitamins A, C, and K, as well as antioxidants.

- **Avocado**: Avocado contains glutathione, a potent antioxidant that aids in liver detoxification. It also provides healthy fats and essential nutrients for overall health.

- **Broccoli**: Broccoli is rich in glucosinolates, sulfur-containing compounds that enhance the liver's detoxification enzymes. It is also high in fiber and antioxidants.

- **Artichokes**: Artichokes support liver function and bile production. They are also rich in fiber and antioxidants, promoting overall health.

- **Turmeric**: Turmeric contains curcumin, which supports liver function and reduces inflammation.

It also has antioxidant properties that enhance overall detoxification.

The Somatic Detox Diet emphasizes the consumption of whole, nutrient-dense foods that support the body's natural detoxification processes. Fruits and vegetables provide essential vitamins, minerals, and antioxidants, while whole grains and legumes offer fiber, protein, and sustained energy. Nuts and seeds supply healthy fats and additional nutrients, and herbs and spices enhance flavor while providing detoxifying properties.

Toxin intake can be decreased, the body's detoxification processes can be supported, and general health can be improved by include a range of these foods in the diet. By stressing the significance of a well-balanced, nutrient-rich diet for optimum health, the Somatic Detox Diet presents a comprehensive approach to detoxification.

Chapter 5: Foods to Avoid

Processed Foods and Refined Sugars

Processed Foods

Processed foods are those that have been altered from their natural state through various methods such as canning, freezing, refrigeration, dehydration, and packaging. These foods often contain added sugars, unhealthy fats, artificial additives, and preservatives, which can hinder the body's natural detoxification processes and contribute to various health issues.

Nutrient Depletion

One of the main problems with processed foods is that they are often stripped of essential nutrients. For example, refining grains removes the bran and germ, which contain fiber, vitamins, and minerals, leaving behind a product that is less nutritious. Similarly, the processing of fruits and vegetables can reduce their vitamin and mineral content. Consuming a diet high in processed foods can lead to nutrient deficiencies, which can impair the body's ability to detoxify effectively.

Added Sugars and Unhealthy Fats

Processed foods often contain high amounts of added sugars and unhealthy fats. Added sugars, such as high fructose corn syrup and cane sugar, provide empty calories and can contribute to weight gain, insulin resistance, and inflammation. Unhealthy fats, such as trans fats and refined vegetable oils, can promote inflammation and increase the risk of chronic diseases like heart disease and diabetes. These components can overwhelm the liver and other detoxification organs, making it harder for the body to eliminate toxins.

Chemical Additives

Many processed foods contain chemical additives such as artificial flavors, colors, and preservatives. These substances can burden the liver and other detoxification organs, as they need to be metabolized and eliminated from the body. Long-term exposure to these chemicals can contribute to toxic buildup and negatively impact overall health.

Refined Sugars

Refined sugars are simple carbohydrates that have been processed to remove impurities and nutrients. Common sources include table sugar, high fructose corn syrup, and corn syrup. These sugars are quickly absorbed into the bloodstream, causing rapid spikes in blood sugar levels followed by crashes. This can lead to insulin resistance, weight gain, and increased inflammation, all of which can hinder detoxification.

Impact on Liver Function

The liver is a primary organ involved in detoxification, and it relies on a steady supply of nutrients to function effectively. Consuming high amounts of refined sugars can overwhelm the liver and contribute to fatty liver disease, a condition in which fat builds up in the liver and impairs its ability to detoxify. This can lead to a reduced capacity to eliminate toxins and an increased risk of chronic diseases.

Promoting Inflammation

Refined sugars can promote inflammation throughout the body. Chronic inflammation is associated with numerous health issues, including heart disease, diabetes, and autoimmune disorders. Inflammation can also impair the function of detoxification organs, making it harder for the body to eliminate toxins.

Caffeine and Alcohol

Caffeine

Caffeine is a stimulant found in coffee, tea, energy drinks, and some medications. While moderate consumption of caffeine can have some health benefits, excessive intake can have negative effects on the body's detoxification processes.

Impact on Liver Function

The liver metabolizes caffeine, and excessive consumption can burden this organ, impairing its ability to detoxify other substances. High caffeine intake can also lead to the depletion of essential nutrients, such as magnesium and B vitamins, which are necessary for liver function and detoxification.

Adrenal Fatigue

Caffeine stimulates the adrenal glands to produce stress hormones like cortisol and adrenaline. Chronic caffeine consumption can lead to adrenal fatigue, a condition in which the adrenal glands become overworked and unable to produce adequate amounts of these hormones. This can lead to chronic fatigue, reduced immune function, and impaired detoxification.

Disrupted Sleep

Caffeine can interfere with sleep patterns, leading to poor quality sleep or insomnia. Adequate sleep is essential for the body's natural detoxification processes, as it is during sleep that the body repairs itself and eliminates toxins. Disrupted sleep can hinder these processes and negatively impact overall health.

Alcohol

Alcohol is a central nervous system depressant that is metabolized by the liver. While moderate alcohol consumption may have some health benefits, excessive intake can have serious negative effects on the body's detoxification processes.

Impact on Liver Function

The liver is responsible for metabolizing alcohol, and excessive consumption can overwhelm this organ, leading to conditions such as fatty liver disease, alcoholic hepatitis, and cirrhosis. These conditions impair the liver's ability to detoxify other substances and can lead to toxic buildup in the body.

Nutrient Depletion

Alcohol consumption can deplete the body of essential nutrients, such as vitamins A, B, C, and E, as well as minerals like magnesium, zinc, and selenium. These nutrients are necessary for detoxification and overall health. Nutrient deficiencies can impair the function of detoxification organs and increase the risk of chronic diseases.

Dehydration

Alcohol is a diuretic, meaning it increases urine production and can lead to dehydration. Adequate hydration is essential for detoxification, as water helps flush toxins from the body. Dehydration can impair the function of detoxification organs and hinder the elimination of toxins.

Artificial Additives and Preservatives

Artificial Additives

Artificial additives, including artificial flavors, colors, and sweeteners, are commonly found in processed foods. These substances are added to enhance the taste, appearance, and shelf life of foods but can have negative effects on health and detoxification.

Impact on Liver Function

The liver is responsible for metabolizing and eliminating artificial additives from the body. Excessive consumption of these substances can burden the liver and impair its ability to detoxify other substances. This can lead to toxic buildup and negatively impact overall health.

Allergic Reactions and Sensitivities

Some people may have allergic reactions or sensitivities to artificial additives. Symptoms can include headaches, digestive issues, skin rashes, and respiratory problems. These reactions can stress the body's detoxification systems and contribute to inflammation.

Preservatives

Preservatives are chemicals added to foods to prevent spoilage and extend shelf life. Common preservatives include sulfites, nitrates, and benzoates. While these substances can help keep foods fresh, they can also have negative effects on health.

Sulfites

Sulfites are commonly used as preservatives in processed foods and beverages, such as dried fruits, wine, and processed meats. Some people are sensitive to sulfites and may experience symptoms such as headaches, hives, and asthma-like symptoms. Sulfites can also deplete the body of essential nutrients, such as vitamin B1 (thiamine), which is necessary for detoxification.

Nitrates and Nitrites

Nitrates and nitrites are used as preservatives in processed meats, such as bacon, sausages, and hot dogs. These substances can convert into nitrosamines, which are potentially carcinogenic compounds. Consuming high amounts of nitrates and nitrites can increase the risk of cancer and negatively impact overall health.

Common Allergens and Irritants

Gluten

Gluten is a protein found in wheat, barley, and rye. Some people are sensitive to gluten or have celiac disease, an autoimmune condition in which the ingestion of gluten leads to damage to the small intestine. Consuming gluten can cause symptoms such as digestive issues, headaches, fatigue, and joint pain in sensitive individuals. Avoiding gluten can help reduce inflammation and support the body's detoxification processes.

Dairy

Dairy products, such as milk, cheese, and yogurt, can cause digestive issues, respiratory problems, and skin rashes in some people. Lactose intolerance, a condition in which the body is unable to digest lactose (a sugar found in dairy), is common. Additionally, dairy can be a source of hormones and antibiotics, which can burden the body's detoxification systems. Avoiding dairy can help reduce inflammation and support overall health.

Soy

Soy is a common allergen and can cause symptoms such as digestive issues, headaches, and skin rashes in sensitive individuals. Soy is also a source of phytoestrogens, which can disrupt hormonal balance in some people. Avoiding soy can help reduce inflammation and support the body's detoxification processes.

Artificial Sweeteners

Artificial sweeteners, such as aspartame, sucralose, and saccharin, are commonly used as sugar substitutes in processed foods and beverages. These substances can cause digestive issues, headaches, and allergic reactions in some people. They can also disrupt the balance of the gut microbiome, which is essential for overall health and detoxification. Avoiding artificial sweeteners can help reduce inflammation and support the body's natural detoxification processes.

Processed Meats

Processed meats, such as sausages, hot dogs, and deli meats, are often high in unhealthy fats, sodium, and chemical additives. These meats can promote inflammation, increase the risk of chronic diseases, and burden the body's detoxification systems. Avoiding processed meats can help reduce the intake of harmful substances and support overall health.

The Somatic Detox Diet emphasizes the avoidance of certain foods and substances that can hinder the body's natural detoxification processes and negatively impact overall health. Processed foods and refined sugars, caffeine and alcohol, artificial additives and preservatives, and common allergens and irritants can all contribute to toxic buildup, inflammation, and impaired detoxification.

By eliminating these foods from the diet, individuals can reduce their exposure to harmful substances, support the body's natural detoxification pathways, and promote overall health and well-being. The Somatic Detox Diet offers a holistic approach to detoxification, emphasizing the importance of a balanced and nutrient-rich diet for optimal health.

Chapter 6: Meal Planning and Recipes

Weekly Meal Planning Strategies

Effective meal planning is crucial for the success of the Somatic Detox Diet. It helps ensure that you have nutritious, detox-friendly meals ready throughout the week, reduces the likelihood of making unhealthy food choices, and saves time and money. Here are some key strategies for planning your meals:

1. Assess Your Dietary Needs and Preferences

Before you begin meal planning, it's essential to understand your dietary needs and preferences. Consider any food allergies, intolerances, or dietary restrictions you may have, such as gluten-free, dairy-free, vegetarian, or vegan. Also, take into account your daily calorie requirements, which can vary based on age, gender, activity level, and overall health.

2. Plan Balanced Meals

Each meal should include a balance of macronutrients: carbohydrates, proteins, and fats. Aim to incorporate a variety of whole foods, including fruits, vegetables, whole grains, legumes, nuts, seeds, and lean proteins. This ensures you get a wide range of essential nutrients that support detoxification and overall health.

3. Prepare a Weekly Menu

Create a weekly menu that outlines what you will eat for breakfast, lunch, dinner, and snacks each day. This helps you stay organized and ensures you have all the ingredients you need. Consider themes for each day to simplify planning, such as Meatless Monday, Taco Tuesday, or Soup and Salad Saturday.

4. Make a Shopping List

Once you have your weekly menu, make a detailed shopping list of all the ingredients you will need. Organize your list by sections of the grocery store (produce, grains, dairy, etc.) to make shopping more efficient. Stick to your list to avoid impulse buys and ensure you have everything necessary for your planned meals.

5. Batch Cooking and Meal Prep

Set aside time each week for batch cooking and meal prep. Prepare large quantities of staples like grains, legumes, roasted vegetables, and proteins that can be used in multiple meals. Portion out meals into containers for easy grab-and-go options throughout the week. This saves time and ensures you have healthy meals readily available.

6. Flexibility and Variety

While it's important to have a plan, be flexible and open to making adjustments as needed. Incorporate a variety of foods to prevent boredom and ensure you get a broad spectrum of nutrients. Experiment with new recipes and ingredients to keep meals exciting and enjoyable.

Sample Meal Plans for Different Dietary Preferences

Here are sample meal plans for vegetarian, vegan, and omnivore dietary preferences, providing a variety of detox-friendly options for each meal.

Vegetarian Meal Plan

Breakfast:

- Green Smoothie Bowl: Blend spinach, banana, almond milk, and chia seeds. Top with granola, berries, and a drizzle of honey.

Lunch:

- Quinoa Salad: Mix cooked quinoa with cherry tomatoes, cucumber, red onion, chickpeas, and feta cheese. Toss with lemon-tahini dressing.

Dinner:

- Stuffed Bell Peppers: Fill bell peppers with a mixture of brown rice, black beans, corn, diced tomatoes, and spices. Top with shredded cheese and bake.

Snack:

- Hummus and Veggie Sticks: Serve homemade hummus with carrot sticks, celery, and bell pepper slices.

Vegan Meal Plan

Breakfast:

- Overnight Oats: Combine rolled oats, chia seeds, almond milk, and a splash of vanilla extract. Top with sliced banana and almond butter.

Lunch:

- Lentil Soup: Cook lentils with diced carrots, celery, onion, garlic, and vegetable broth. Season with cumin and turmeric.

Dinner:

- Vegetable Stir-Fry: Sauté broccoli, bell peppers, snap peas, and tofu in a garlic-ginger sauce. Serve over brown rice.

Snack:

- Trail Mix: Mix raw almonds, walnuts, pumpkin seeds, dried cranberries, and dark chocolate chips.

Omnivore Meal Plan

Breakfast:

- Scrambled Eggs with Spinach: Sauté spinach in olive oil, then scramble with eggs. Serve with whole grain toast.

Lunch:

- Grilled Chicken Salad: Top mixed greens with grilled chicken breast, avocado, cherry tomatoes, cucumber, and a balsamic vinaigrette.

Dinner:

- Baked Salmon: Season salmon fillets with lemon, dill, and olive oil. Bake and serve with roasted sweet potatoes and steamed asparagus.

Snack:

- Greek Yogurt with Berries: Serve plain Greek yogurt topped with fresh berries and a sprinkle of flaxseeds.

Breakfast, Lunch, Dinner, and Snack Recipes

Here are detailed recipes for each meal, providing delicious and nutritious options that align with the principles of the Somatic Detox Diet.

Breakfast Recipes

Green Smoothie Bowl

Ingredients:

- 1 cup spinach
- 1 banana
- 1 cup almond milk
- 1 tablespoon chia seeds
- Granola (for topping)
- Fresh berries (for topping)
- Honey (optional, for drizzling)

Instructions:

1. Blend the spinach, banana, almond milk, and chia seeds until smooth.
2. Pour the smoothie into a bowl.
3. Top with granola, fresh berries, and a drizzle of honey if desired.

Overnight Oats

Ingredients:

- 1/2 cup rolled oats
- 1 tablespoon chia seeds
- 1 cup almond milk
- 1/2 teaspoon vanilla extract
- 1 banana, sliced
- 1 tablespoon almond butter

Instructions:

1. Combine the rolled oats, chia seeds, almond milk, and vanilla extract in a jar or container.
2. Stir well, cover, and refrigerate overnight.
3. In the morning, top with sliced banana and almond butter.

Scrambled Eggs with Spinach

Ingredients:

- 2 cups fresh spinach

- 2 teaspoons olive oil
- 4 eggs
- Salt and pepper to taste
- Whole grain toast (optional, for serving)

Instructions:

1. Heat the olive oil in a skillet over medium heat.
2. Add the spinach and sauté until wilted.
3. Beat the eggs in a bowl and pour into the skillet with the spinach.
4. Cook, stirring frequently, until the eggs are scrambled and cooked through.
5. Season with salt and pepper. Serve with whole grain toast if desired.

Lunch Recipes

Quinoa Salad

Ingredients:

- 1 cup cooked quinoa
- 1 cup cherry tomatoes, halved
- 1 cucumber, diced
- 1/2 red onion, finely chopped
- 1 cup chickpeas, drained and rinsed
- 1/2 cup feta cheese, crumbled
- Lemon-tahini dressing (see below)

Lemon-Tahini Dressing:

- 1/4 cup tahini
- 1/4 cup lemon juice
- 2 tablespoons olive oil
- 1 tablespoon maple syrup
- 1 garlic clove, minced

- Salt and pepper to taste

Instructions:

1. In a large bowl, combine the cooked quinoa, cherry tomatoes, cucumber, red onion, chickpeas, and feta cheese.

2. In a separate bowl, whisk together the tahini, lemon juice, olive oil, maple syrup, minced garlic, salt, and pepper until smooth.

3. Pour the dressing over the salad and toss to coat evenly.

Lentil Soup

Ingredients:

- 1 cup lentils, rinsed
- 1 onion, diced
- 2 carrots, diced
- 2 celery stalks, diced

- 2 garlic cloves, minced
- 1 teaspoon cumin
- 1 teaspoon turmeric
- 6 cups vegetable broth
- Salt and pepper to taste

Instructions:

1. In a large pot, sauté the onion, carrots, celery, and garlic until softened.
2. Add the lentils, cumin, turmeric, and vegetable broth.
3. Bring to a boil, then reduce heat and simmer for 25-30 minutes, or until the lentils are tender.
4. Season with salt and pepper to taste.

Grilled Chicken Salad

Ingredients:

- 2 cups mixed greens
- 1 grilled chicken breast, sliced
- 1 avocado, sliced
- 1 cup cherry tomatoes, halved
- 1 cucumber, sliced
- Balsamic vinaigrette (see below)

Balsamic Vinaigrette:

- 1/4 cup balsamic vinegar
- 1/4 cup olive oil
- 1 tablespoon Dijon mustard
- 1 tablespoon honey
- Salt and pepper to taste

Instructions:

1. In a large bowl, combine the mixed greens, grilled chicken breast, avocado, cherry tomatoes, and cucumber.

2. In a separate bowl, whisk together the balsamic vinegar, olive oil, Dijon mustard, honey, salt, and pepper until well combined.

3. Drizzle the vinaigrette over the salad and toss to coat evenly.

Dinner Recipes

Stuffed Bell Peppers

Ingredients:

- 4 bell peppers, tops cut off and seeds removed
- 1 cup cooked brown rice
- 1 cup black beans, drained and rinsed
- 1 cup corn kernels
- 1 cup diced tomatoes

- 1 teaspoon cumin
- 1 teaspoon chili powder
- 1/2 cup shredded cheese (optional)

Instructions:

1. Preheat the oven to 375°F (190°C).
2. In a large bowl, combine the cooked brown rice, black beans, corn, diced tomatoes, cumin, and chili powder.
3. Stuff each bell pepper with the rice mixture and place them in a baking dish.
4. Top with shredded cheese if desired.
5. Bake for 25-30 minutes, or until the peppers are tender and the filling is heated through.

Vegetable Stir-Fry

Ingredients:

- 2 cups broccoli florets

- 1 red bell pepper, sliced
- 1 cup snap peas
- 1 cup cubed tofu
- 2 tablespoons olive oil
- 2 garlic cloves, minced
- 1 tablespoon fresh ginger, grated
- 3 tablespoons soy sauce or tamari
- 1 tablespoon sesame oil
- Cooked brown rice (for serving)

Instructions:

1. Heat the olive oil in a large skillet or wok over medium-high heat.
2. Add the garlic and ginger, and sauté for 1-2 minutes until fragrant.
3. Add the broccoli, bell pepper, snap peas, and tofu to the skillet.

4. Cook, stirring frequently, until the vegetables are tender-crisp and the tofu is golden brown.

5. Stir in the soy sauce and sesame oil.

6. Serve over cooked brown rice.

Baked Salmon

Ingredients:

- 4 salmon fillets
- 2 tablespoons olive oil
- 2 tablespoons lemon juice
- 1 teaspoon dried dill
- Salt and pepper to taste
- Roasted sweet potatoes (for serving)
- Steamed asparagus (for serving)

Instructions:

1. Preheat the oven to 400°F (200°C).

2. Place the salmon fillets on a baking sheet lined with parchment paper.

3. Drizzle the olive oil and lemon juice over the salmon fillets.

4. Sprinkle with dried dill, salt, and pepper.

5. Bake for 15-20 minutes, or until the salmon is cooked through and flakes easily with a fork.

6. Serve with roasted sweet potatoes and steamed asparagus.

Snack Recipes

Hummus and Veggie Sticks

Ingredients:

- 1 can chickpeas, drained and rinsed
- 1/4 cup tahini
- 2 tablespoons olive oil
- 2 tablespoons lemon juice

- 2 garlic cloves, minced
- Salt and pepper to taste
- Carrot sticks, celery, and bell pepper slices (for serving)

Instructions:

1. In a food processor, combine the chickpeas, tahini, olive oil, lemon juice, minced garlic, salt, and pepper.
2. Blend until smooth, adding a bit of water if needed to reach the desired consistency.
3. Serve the hummus with carrot sticks, celery, and bell pepper slices.

Trail Mix

Ingredients:

- 1/2 cup raw almonds
- 1/2 cup walnuts

- 1/2 cup pumpkin seeds
- 1/2 cup dried cranberries
- 1/2 cup dark chocolate chips

Instructions:

1. In a large bowl, combine the almonds, walnuts, pumpkin seeds, dried cranberries, and dark chocolate chips.
2. Mix well and store in an airtight container.

Greek Yogurt with Berries

Ingredients:

- 1 cup plain Greek yogurt
- 1/2 cup fresh berries (blueberries, strawberries, raspberries)
- 1 tablespoon flaxseeds

Instructions:

1. Spoon the Greek yogurt into a bowl.

2. Top with fresh berries and a sprinkle of flaxseeds.

Tips for Preparing and Storing Meals

1. Batch Cooking

Batch cooking involves preparing large quantities of food at once, which can be portioned out and stored for later use. This method saves time and ensures you have healthy meals ready throughout the week. Cook staples like grains, legumes, and roasted vegetables in bulk and store them in the refrigerator or freezer.

2. Use Airtight Containers

Store your prepared meals in airtight containers to keep them fresh and prevent spoilage. Glass containers are an excellent choice as they are durable, non-toxic, and can be easily reheated in the microwave or oven.

3. Label and Date

Label each container with the contents and the date it was prepared. This helps you keep track of what needs to be consumed first and reduces food waste.

4. Portion Control

Divide your meals into individual portions to make it easier to grab a healthy meal on the go. This also helps with portion control and prevents overeating.

5. Freezing Meals

Many meals can be frozen for longer storage. Soups, stews, casseroles, and cooked grains freeze well. Allow the food to cool completely before transferring it to freezer-safe containers. Label and date the containers, and use the meals within three months for the best quality.

6. Reheating Tips

When reheating meals, use the microwave, oven, or stovetop as appropriate. Add a splash of water or broth to prevent dishes from drying out. Reheat food to an internal temperature of 165°F (74°C) to ensure it is safe to eat.

7. Plan for Leftovers

Incorporate leftovers into your meal plan to minimize food waste. For example, use leftover roasted vegetables in a salad or stir-fry, or repurpose cooked grains into a new dish.

8. Quick and Easy Snacks

Keep healthy snacks on hand for when you need a quick energy boost. Pre-cut vegetables, portion out nuts and seeds, and prepare small containers of hummus or Greek yogurt for easy access.

9. Use Fresh Herbs and Spices

Enhance the flavor of your meals with fresh herbs and spices. They add variety and can make simple dishes more exciting. Store fresh herbs in a glass of water in the refrigerator to keep them fresh longer.

10. Stay Organized

Keep your kitchen organized and well-stocked with essential ingredients. This makes meal preparation more efficient and enjoyable. Regularly clean out your pantry, refrigerator, and freezer to ensure you are using fresh ingredients.

Meal planning and preparation are essential components of the Somatic Detox Diet. By following weekly meal planning strategies, you can ensure you have nutritious, detox-friendly meals ready throughout the week. Sample meal plans for vegetarian, vegan, and omnivore preferences provide a variety of options to suit different dietary needs. Detailed recipes for breakfast, lunch, dinner, and snacks offer delicious and nutritious choices that align with the principles of the Somatic Detox Diet.

By incorporating tips for preparing and storing meals, you can save time, reduce food waste, and ensure you always have healthy options available. The Somatic Detox Diet emphasizes the importance of a balanced and nutrient-rich diet, and effective meal planning and preparation are key to achieving and maintaining optimal health and well-being.

Chapter 7: The Role of Supplements and Herbal Remedies

Overview of Beneficial Supplements

In the context of the Somatic Detox Diet, supplements can play a supportive role by providing additional nutrients that may be lacking in the diet and enhancing the body's natural detoxification processes. However, it is essential to approach supplementation with caution and prioritize obtaining nutrients from whole foods whenever possible. Below is an overview of beneficial supplements that can support detoxification:

1. Multivitamins

A high-quality multivitamin can help fill nutritional gaps in the diet, ensuring that the body receives a broad spectrum of essential vitamins and minerals. These micronutrients are crucial for various metabolic processes, including detoxification.

2. Probiotics

Probiotics are beneficial bacteria that support gut health. A healthy gut microbiome is essential for effective detoxification, as it aids in digestion, enhances nutrient absorption, and helps eliminate toxins. Probiotic supplements can help restore and maintain a balanced gut flora, especially after antibiotic use or during times of stress.

3. Omega-3 Fatty Acids

Omega-3 fatty acids, found in fish oil and flaxseed oil supplements, have anti-inflammatory properties that support overall health. They play a vital role in reducing inflammation, which can impede detoxification. Omega-3 supplements can also support liver function and improve cell membrane integrity.

4. Vitamin C

Vitamin C is a powerful antioxidant that supports the immune system and aids in the neutralization of free radicals. It also enhances the body's detoxification pathways by boosting the production of glutathione, a key antioxidant involved in liver detoxification.

5. Milk Thistle

Milk thistle is a well-known herb used to support liver health. The active compound, silymarin, has antioxidant and anti-inflammatory properties that protect liver cells from damage and enhance liver regeneration. Milk thistle supplements can support liver function and promote detoxification.

6. N-Acetyl Cysteine (NAC)

NAC is a precursor to glutathione, one of the body's most important antioxidants. Supplementing with NAC can help boost glutathione levels, enhancing the liver's ability to detoxify harmful substances. NAC also supports respiratory health and reduces oxidative stress.

7. Activated Charcoal

Activated charcoal is a natural adsorbent that can bind to toxins and help eliminate them from the body. It is commonly used in cases of acute poisoning but can also be used in smaller doses to support general detoxification. However, it should be used with caution and not taken with medications or essential nutrients, as it can interfere with their absorption.

8. Fiber Supplements

Fiber is essential for digestive health and detoxification. It helps bind to toxins in the digestive tract and facilitates their elimination through bowel movements. While it is best to obtain fiber from whole foods, fiber supplements like psyllium husk or inulin can be beneficial for those who need additional support.

Herbal Remedies and Their Detoxifying Properties

Herbal remedies have been used for centuries to support detoxification and overall health. Many herbs possess properties that enhance the body's natural detoxification pathways, reduce inflammation, and support organ function. Below are some herbal remedies commonly used in the Somatic Detox Diet:

1. Dandelion Root

Dandelion root is known for its liver-supporting properties. It stimulates bile production, aiding in the digestion and elimination of fats and toxins. Dandelion root also acts as a diuretic, promoting kidney function and helping to eliminate excess fluids and waste products from the body.

2. Turmeric

Turmeric contains curcumin, a powerful anti-inflammatory and antioxidant compound. Curcumin supports liver health by enhancing detoxification enzymes and reducing oxidative stress. Turmeric also has anti-inflammatory properties that can reduce systemic inflammation and support overall health.

3. Ginger

Ginger is a well-known digestive aid that can help relieve nausea, bloating, and indigestion. It has anti-inflammatory and antioxidant properties that support liver function and enhance detoxification. Ginger also promotes circulation, which can help distribute nutrients and remove waste products more efficiently.

4. Burdock Root

Burdock root has been traditionally used as a blood purifier. It supports liver and kidney function, helping to remove toxins from the blood. Burdock root also has diuretic properties, promoting the elimination of waste products through urine. Additionally, it contains antioxidants that protect cells from damage.

5. Cilantro

Cilantro is known for its ability to bind to heavy metals and facilitate their elimination from the body. It contains compounds that enhance the body's natural detoxification pathways and support liver function.

Cilantro is often used in combination with other detoxifying herbs to enhance its effectiveness.

6. Parsley

Parsley is a nutrient-dense herb that supports kidney function and acts as a natural diuretic. It helps eliminate excess fluids and waste products from the body. Parsley also contains antioxidants and anti-inflammatory compounds that support overall health and detoxification.

7. Nettle

Nettle is a versatile herb that supports kidney function and acts as a natural diuretic. It helps eliminate excess fluids and waste products from the body. Nettle is also rich in vitamins and minerals, including iron, which supports overall health and energy levels.

8. Milk Thistle

As mentioned earlier, milk thistle is a powerful herb for liver support. Its active compound, silymarin, protects liver cells from damage, enhances liver regeneration, and supports detoxification. Milk thistle is commonly used in detox programs to promote liver health.

How to Safely Incorporate Supplements into the Diet

Incorporating supplements into the diet can provide additional support for detoxification, but it is essential to do so safely and thoughtfully. Here are some guidelines for incorporating supplements into the Somatic Detox Diet:

1. Consult with a Healthcare Professional

Before starting any new supplement regimen, it is crucial to consult with a healthcare professional, such as a doctor or registered dietitian. They can help determine which supplements are appropriate for your individual needs and ensure there are no potential interactions with medications or existing health conditions.

2. Choose High-Quality Supplements

Not all supplements are created equal. Choose high-quality supplements from reputable brands that undergo third-party testing for purity and potency. Look for supplements that are free from fillers, artificial additives, and contaminants.

3. Follow Recommended Dosages

Always follow the recommended dosages provided by the manufacturer or healthcare professional. Taking more than the recommended dose can lead to adverse effects and may not provide additional benefits. Be mindful of the cumulative intake of certain nutrients if taking multiple supplements.

4. Incorporate Supplements into a Balanced Diet

Supplements should complement a balanced diet, not replace whole foods. Focus on obtaining nutrients from a variety of whole foods, including fruits, vegetables, whole grains, legumes, nuts, seeds, and lean proteins. Use supplements to fill specific nutritional gaps or provide additional support as needed.

5. Monitor for Adverse Effects

Pay attention to how your body responds to supplements. If you experience any adverse effects, such as digestive issues, headaches, or allergic reactions, discontinue use and consult with a healthcare professional. They can help identify the cause and recommend alternative options if necessary.

6. Timing and Absorption

Certain supplements are better absorbed when taken with food, while others may need to be taken on an empty stomach. Follow the instructions on the supplement label or consult with a healthcare professional for guidance on the best timing for optimal absorption.

7. Stay Hydrated

Many supplements, especially those that support detoxification, require adequate hydration to be effective. Drink plenty of water throughout the day to support the body's natural detoxification processes and enhance the effectiveness of supplements.

Precautions and Contraindications

While supplements and herbal remedies can provide significant benefits, it is essential to be aware of potential precautions and contraindications. Here are some considerations to keep in mind:

1. Potential Interactions with Medications

Some supplements and herbal remedies can interact with medications, affecting their efficacy or causing adverse effects. For example, St. John's Wort can interact with antidepressants, and garlic supplements can affect blood-thinning medications. Always consult with a healthcare professional before starting any new supplement, especially if you are taking prescription medications.

2. Allergies and Sensitivities

Be aware of any allergies or sensitivities to specific supplements or herbs. For example, individuals with ragweed allergies may also be sensitive to chamomile. If you have a history of allergies, it is essential to check the ingredients and consult with a healthcare professional before using a new supplement or herbal remedy.

3. Pregnancy and Breastfeeding

Certain supplements and herbal remedies may not be safe for use during pregnancy or breastfeeding. For example, high doses of vitamin A can be harmful to a developing fetus, and some herbs, such as black cohosh, may stimulate uterine contractions. Pregnant and breastfeeding individuals should consult with a healthcare professional before using any supplements or herbal remedies.

4. Pre-Existing Health Conditions

Individuals with pre-existing health conditions, such as liver or kidney disease, should exercise caution when using supplements and herbal remedies. Some supplements can place additional strain on these organs and exacerbate existing conditions. Consult with a healthcare professional to determine the safety and appropriateness of supplements for your specific health needs.

5. Quality and Purity

The quality and purity of supplements and herbal remedies can vary widely. Contaminated or adulterated products can pose serious health risks. Choose supplements from reputable brands that undergo third-party testing for purity and potency. Avoid products with unknown or questionable ingredients.

6. Overconsumption

Taking excessive amounts of certain supplements can lead to toxicity and adverse effects. For example, high doses of vitamin D can cause hypercalcemia, and excessive iron intake can lead to iron toxicity. Always follow the recommended dosages and consult with a healthcare professional if you are unsure.

7. Duration of Use

Some supplements and herbal remedies are intended for short-term use only. Prolonged use of certain herbs, such as licorice root, can lead to adverse effects like hypertension. Follow the guidelines provided by the manufacturer or healthcare professional regarding the duration of use.

The role of supplements and herbal remedies in the Somatic Detox Diet is to provide additional support for the body's natural detoxification processes. Beneficial supplements, such as multivitamins, probiotics, omega-3 fatty acids, and milk thistle, can help fill nutritional gaps and enhance detoxification. Herbal remedies, including dandelion root, turmeric, ginger, and burdock root, offer natural detoxifying properties and support overall health.

Incorporating supplements and herbal remedies safely into the diet requires careful consideration, consultation with healthcare professionals, and attention to quality and dosages. Being aware of potential precautions and contraindications is essential to avoid adverse effects and ensure the effectiveness of the detoxification process.

By thoughtfully integrating supplements and herbal remedies into the Somatic Detox Diet, individuals can enhance their body's ability to detoxify, reduce exposure to harmful substances, and promote overall health and well-being.

Chapter 8: Hydration and Detoxification

Importance of Water in the Detox Process

Water is essential for life and plays a critical role in nearly every bodily function, including detoxification. Proper hydration is fundamental to the Somatic Detox Diet because it supports the body's natural detox processes by facilitating the elimination of waste products and toxins.

1. Supporting Kidney Function

The kidneys are primary organs of detoxification. They filter blood to remove waste products and excess substances, which are then excreted as urine. Adequate water intake is crucial for maintaining kidney health and ensuring efficient filtration. Dehydration can lead to the buildup of waste products and increase the risk of kidney stones and urinary tract infections.

2. Assisting Liver Detoxification

The liver is another vital detoxification organ. It processes toxins, drugs, and metabolic waste, converting them into water-soluble substances that can be excreted via urine or bile. Water is necessary for the liver to perform these functions effectively. It helps maintain blood volume and pressure, ensuring that the liver receives an adequate supply of blood to filter and detoxify.

3. Promoting Digestive Health

Water aids in digestion by helping break down food and absorb nutrients. It also softens stool, preventing constipation and promoting regular bowel movements. Efficient digestion and elimination are essential for removing toxins and waste products from the body. Dehydration can lead to digestive issues and impede the body's ability to detoxify.

4. Facilitating Sweating

Sweating is a natural detoxification process where the body expels toxins through the skin. Adequate hydration is necessary to support sweating, especially during physical activity or in hot environments. Sweating helps regulate body temperature and remove substances like heavy metals and metabolic waste from the body.

5. Maintaining Cellular Health

Water is essential for maintaining cellular health and function. It is involved in numerous biochemical reactions within cells, including those related to detoxification. Proper hydration ensures that cells can perform these functions efficiently, supporting overall health and detoxification.

Recommended Daily Water Intake

Determining the right amount of water intake can vary based on several factors, including age, gender, activity level, climate, and overall health. Here are general guidelines for daily water intake:

1. General Recommendations

- For adults, a common recommendation is to drink at least 8-10 8-ounce glasses of water per day, which equals about 2-2.5 liters or half a gallon.

- Another guideline is to drink half your body weight in ounces. For example, if you weigh 150 pounds, you should aim to drink 75 ounces of water daily.

- The Institute of Medicine (IOM) recommends a total daily water intake of about 3.7 liters (125 ounces) for men and 2.7 liters (91 ounces) for women, including all beverages and water-rich foods.

2. Adjustments Based on Activity and Environment

- Increased Physical Activity: If you engage in regular physical activity, you may need more water to compensate for fluid loss through sweat.

It's important to drink water before, during, and after exercise.

- Hot or Humid Climates: In hot or humid climates, you lose more water through sweat, so it's essential to increase your water intake to stay hydrated.

- Health Conditions: Certain health conditions, such as kidney stones or urinary tract infections, may require higher water intake. Always consult with a healthcare professional for personalized recommendations.

3. Signs of Adequate Hydration

- Clear or Light-Colored Urine: Dark yellow or amber-colored urine can be a sign of dehydration.

- Regular Urination: You should be urinating every few hours. Infrequent urination can indicate inadequate fluid intake.

- Lack of Thirst: Feeling thirsty is a sign that your body needs more water. Aim to drink water consistently throughout the day to avoid thirst.

Detoxifying Beverages

In addition to plain water, there are various detoxifying beverages that can enhance hydration and support the body's detox processes. These include herbal teas, infused waters, and other natural drinks with beneficial properties.

1. Herbal Teas

Herbal teas are an excellent way to increase fluid intake while providing additional detoxifying benefits. Some popular detoxifying herbal teas include:

- **Dandelion Root Tea**: Dandelion root supports liver function and stimulates bile production, aiding in the digestion and elimination of fats and toxins.

- **Milk Thistle Tea**: Milk thistle contains silymarin, which protects liver cells and enhances liver detoxification.

- **Ginger Tea**: Ginger has anti-inflammatory and antioxidant properties that support digestion and detoxification.

- **Green Tea**: Green tea is rich in catechins, antioxidants that enhance liver function and support detoxification.

2. Infused Waters

Infused waters are made by adding fruits, vegetables, and herbs to water, infusing it with flavors and beneficial compounds. Here are some popular combinations:

- **Lemon and Mint**: Lemon provides vitamin C and antioxidants, while mint aids digestion and provides a refreshing taste.

- **Cucumber and Basil**: Cucumber is hydrating and anti-inflammatory, and basil offers antioxidants and supports digestion.

- **Orange and Blueberry**: Oranges are rich in vitamin C, and blueberries provide antioxidants and anti-inflammatory properties.

- **Strawberry and Rosemary**: Strawberries are high in antioxidants, and rosemary supports liver function and digestion.

3. Natural Detox Drinks

Natural detox drinks combine various ingredients known for their detoxifying properties. Here are some examples:

- **Apple Cider Vinegar Drink**: Mix 1-2 tablespoons of apple cider vinegar with a glass of water. Add a teaspoon of honey and a dash of cinnamon for taste. Apple cider vinegar supports digestion and helps balance pH levels.

- **Turmeric and Lemon Water**: Mix the juice of half a lemon with a teaspoon of turmeric powder in warm water. Add a pinch of black pepper to enhance absorption. Turmeric has powerful anti-inflammatory and antioxidant properties.

- **Aloe Vera Juice**: Aloe vera juice supports digestion and has detoxifying properties. Mix aloe vera gel with water and a splash of lemon juice for a refreshing drink.

Recipes for Detox Drinks

Here are detailed recipes for various detox drinks that can be incorporated into the Somatic Detox Diet:

1. Lemon and Mint Infused Water

Ingredients:

- 1 lemon, sliced
- 10-12 fresh mint leaves
- 1-liter water

Instructions:

1. Add the lemon slices and mint leaves to a pitcher of water.

2. Let it sit in the refrigerator for at least 2 hours, or overnight, to allow the flavors to infuse.

3. Serve chilled and enjoy throughout the day.

2. Dandelion Root Tea

Ingredients:

- 1 tablespoon dried dandelion root
- 1 cup boiling water
- Honey or lemon (optional, for taste)

Instructions:

1. Place the dried dandelion root in a teapot or mug.

2. Pour boiling water over the dandelion root and let it steep for 10-15 minutes.

3. Strain the tea and add honey or lemon if desired.

4. Drink warm.

3. Cucumber and Basil Infused Water

Ingredients:

- 1 cucumber, sliced
- 10-12 fresh basil leaves
- 1-liter water

Instructions:

1. Add the cucumber slices and basil leaves to a pitcher of water.

2. Let it sit in the refrigerator for at least 2 hours, or overnight, to allow the flavors to infuse.

3. Serve chilled and enjoy throughout the day.

4. Apple Cider Vinegar Drink

Ingredients:

- 1-2 tablespoons apple cider vinegar
- 1 glass of water
- 1 teaspoon honey
- Dash of cinnamon

Instructions:

1. Mix the apple cider vinegar and honey in a glass of water.
2. Add a dash of cinnamon and stir well.
3. Drink before meals to aid digestion and support detoxification.

5. Turmeric and Lemon Water

Ingredients:

- Juice of 1/2 lemon
- 1 teaspoon turmeric powder
- Pinch of black pepper

- Warm water

Instructions:

1. Mix the lemon juice and turmeric powder in a glass of warm water.

2. Add a pinch of black pepper to enhance the absorption of curcumin, the active compound in turmeric.

3. Stir well and drink.

6. Aloe Vera Juice

Ingredients:

- 2 tablespoons aloe vera gel (from fresh aloe vera leaves)
- 1 glass of water
- Splash of lemon juice

Instructions:

1. Extract the gel from fresh aloe vera leaves.

2. Blend the aloe vera gel with a glass of water and a splash of lemon juice.

3. Drink in the morning to support digestion and detoxification.

Hydration is a fundamental aspect of the Somatic Detox Diet and plays a critical role in supporting the body's natural detoxification processes. Water is essential for kidney function, liver detoxification, digestion, sweating, and maintaining cellular health. Adequate hydration ensures that these processes function efficiently, promoting overall health and well-being.

In addition to plain water, detoxifying beverages such as herbal teas, infused waters, and natural detox drinks can enhance hydration and provide additional health benefits. These beverages contain compounds that support liver function, reduce inflammation, aid digestion, and facilitate the elimination of toxins.

Incorporating a variety of detox drinks into your daily routine can make hydration enjoyable and support the detoxification goals of the Somatic Detox Diet. By staying properly hydrated and enjoying these nourishing beverages, you can enhance your body's ability to detoxify and achieve optimal health and well-being.

Chapter 9: Physical Activity and Somatic Detox

The Role of Exercise in Detoxification

Physical activity is a cornerstone of the Somatic Detox Diet, as it significantly enhances the body's natural detoxification processes. Exercise supports detoxification through multiple mechanisms, including promoting circulation, enhancing lymphatic drainage, stimulating sweat production, and improving digestive function.

1. Promoting Circulation

Regular physical activity improves blood circulation, ensuring that oxygen and essential nutrients are efficiently delivered to cells while waste products and toxins are transported to detoxification organs, such as the liver and kidneys, for elimination. Enhanced circulation also supports cardiovascular health and increases overall energy levels.

2. Enhancing Lymphatic Drainage

The lymphatic system is a network of tissues and organs that help rid the body of toxins, waste, and other unwanted materials. Unlike the circulatory system, the lymphatic system does not have a central pump (like the heart) and relies on physical movement to circulate lymph fluid. Exercise, particularly activities that involve rhythmic muscle contractions, such as walking and yoga, can stimulate lymphatic flow and facilitate the removal of toxins.

3. Stimulating Sweat Production

Sweating is a natural detoxification process that helps expel toxins through the skin. Exercise-induced sweating can help eliminate substances such as heavy metals, urea, and lactic acid from the body. Regular physical activity, therefore, supports the detoxification process by promoting sweat production and enhancing skin health.

4. Improving Digestive Function

Physical activity can improve digestive health by stimulating peristalsis, the series of muscle contractions that move food through the digestive tract. Improved digestion supports regular bowel movements, which are essential for eliminating waste and toxins from the body. Exercise also helps prevent constipation, reducing the risk of toxin reabsorption in the colon.

5. Reducing Stress and Inflammation

Chronic stress and inflammation can impair the body's detoxification processes. Exercise is known to reduce stress by releasing endorphins, the body's natural mood elevators, and decreasing levels of cortisol, the stress hormone. Regular physical activity also has anti-inflammatory effects, which can further support detoxification and overall health.

Recommended Types of Physical Activities

The Somatic Detox Diet emphasizes a balanced approach to physical activity, incorporating various types of exercise to support overall well-being and enhance detoxification. Here are some recommended types of physical activities:

1. Yoga

Yoga is a mind-body practice that combines physical postures, breathing exercises, and meditation. It is particularly beneficial for detoxification due to its ability to promote circulation, stimulate lymphatic flow, and enhance mental clarity. Different styles of yoga, such as Hatha, Vinyasa, and Yin yoga, offer various benefits:

- **Hatha Yoga**: Focuses on gentle postures and breathing exercises, making it suitable for beginners and those looking to reduce stress.

- **Vinyasa Yoga**: Involves a series of flowing movements that synchronize with the breath, providing a cardiovascular workout and enhancing flexibility.

- **Yin Yoga**: Emphasizes deep stretching and holding poses for extended periods, which can improve joint health and promote relaxation.

2. Walking

Walking is a low-impact, accessible form of exercise that can be easily incorporated into daily routines. It promotes cardiovascular health, enhances circulation, and stimulates lymphatic drainage. Walking outdoors also provides the added benefit of connecting with nature, which can reduce stress and improve mental well-being.

3. Strength Training

Strength training involves exercises that use resistance to build muscle strength and endurance. It includes activities such as weightlifting, bodyweight exercises, and resistance band workouts. Strength training supports detoxification by:

- **Enhancing Muscle Mass**: Increased muscle mass can improve metabolic rate and support the body's ability to burn calories and eliminate toxins.

- **Supporting Bone Health**: Weight-bearing exercises strengthen bones and reduce the risk of osteoporosis.

- **Improving Insulin Sensitivity**: Strength training can help regulate blood sugar levels, reducing the risk of metabolic disorders that can impair detoxification.

4. Cardiovascular Exercise

Cardiovascular exercise, also known as aerobic exercise, includes activities such as running, cycling, swimming, and dancing. These exercises elevate the heart rate, improve cardiovascular health, and promote sweat production. Cardiovascular exercise supports detoxification by enhancing circulation, increasing lung capacity, and stimulating the release of endorphins.

5. High-Intensity Interval Training (HIIT)

HIIT involves alternating between short bursts of intense exercise and periods of rest or low-intensity activity. This form of exercise can be highly effective for improving cardiovascular fitness, boosting metabolism, and promoting fat loss. HIIT also stimulates sweat production and supports detoxification through its vigorous nature.

Incorporating Mindfulness and Meditation Practices

Mindfulness and meditation are integral components of the Somatic Detox Diet, as they support mental and emotional health, which are essential for effective detoxification. Incorporating these practices into your daily routine can help reduce stress, enhance mental clarity, and promote overall well-being.

1. Mindfulness Meditation

Mindfulness meditation involves paying attention to the present moment without judgment. It can be practiced in various forms, such as sitting meditation, walking meditation, or mindful breathing. Benefits of mindfulness meditation include:

- **Reducing Stress**: Mindfulness meditation can lower cortisol levels and reduce stress, which can enhance the body's detoxification processes.

- **Improving Mental Clarity**: Regular practice can improve focus, concentration, and mental clarity.

- **Enhancing Emotional Resilience**: Mindfulness meditation can help develop emotional resilience and improve overall mental well-being.

2. Guided Imagery

Guided imagery is a relaxation technique that involves visualizing calming and positive images to promote relaxation and reduce stress. This practice can support detoxification by:

- **Promoting Relaxation**: Visualizing peaceful scenes can activate the body's relaxation response, reducing stress and enhancing detoxification.

- **Enhancing Mental Well-Being**: Guided imagery can improve mood and promote a sense of well-being.

3. Deep Breathing Exercises

Deep breathing exercises, such as diaphragmatic breathing or alternate nostril breathing, can support detoxification by:

- **Improving Oxygenation**: Deep breathing increases oxygen intake, which supports cellular function and detoxification.

- **Stimulating the Parasympathetic Nervous System**: Deep breathing activates the parasympathetic nervous system, promoting relaxation and reducing stress.

- **Enhancing Lung Capacity**: Regular practice can improve lung capacity and support respiratory health.

4. Body Scan Meditation

Body scan meditation involves focusing attention on different parts of the body, from the toes to the head, and observing any sensations without judgment. This practice can support detoxification by:

- **Increasing Body Awareness**: Enhancing awareness of physical sensations can help identify areas of tension and stress.
- **Promoting Relaxation**: Focusing on the body can promote relaxation and reduce stress, supporting overall well-being.

Creating a Balanced Routine

A balanced routine that integrates physical activity, mindfulness, and meditation practices is essential for supporting detoxification and overall health. Here are some tips for creating a balanced routine:

1. Set Realistic Goals

Set realistic and achievable goals for your physical activity and mindfulness practices. Consider your current fitness level, lifestyle, and schedule. Start with small, manageable changes and gradually increase the intensity and duration of your activities.

2. Mix Different Types of Activities

Incorporate a variety of physical activities into your routine to ensure a balanced approach. Aim to include cardiovascular exercise, strength training, flexibility exercises, and activities that promote relaxation, such as yoga and mindfulness meditation. This variety can prevent boredom and reduce the risk of overuse injuries.

3. Schedule Regular Workouts

Plan your workouts in advance and schedule them at times that are convenient for you. Consistency is key to reaping the benefits of regular physical activity. Aim for at least 150 minutes of moderate-intensity aerobic exercise or 75 minutes of vigorous-intensity aerobic exercise per week, combined with strength training exercises at least two days per week.

4. Prioritize Rest and Recovery

Rest and recovery are essential components of a balanced routine. Ensure you get adequate sleep each night, as sleep is crucial for the body's detoxification processes. Incorporate rest days into your exercise routine to allow your muscles to recover and prevent burnout.

5. Practice Mindfulness Daily

Incorporate mindfulness practices into your daily routine, even if only for a few minutes each day. Set aside time for meditation, deep breathing exercises, or simply being present in the moment. These practices can help reduce stress, improve mental clarity, and support overall well-being.

6. Listen to Your Body

Pay attention to your body's signals and adjust your routine as needed. If you feel fatigued, sore, or unwell, take a break or modify your activities. Pushing through discomfort can lead to injury and impede your progress.

7. Stay Hydrated

Proper hydration is essential for supporting physical activity and detoxification. Drink plenty of water before, during, and after exercise to stay hydrated and support your body's detox processes.

8. Seek Professional Guidance

If you are new to exercise or mindfulness practices, consider seeking guidance from a fitness professional, yoga instructor, or meditation teacher. They can provide personalized recommendations and ensure you practice safely and effectively.

Physical activity and mindfulness practices are integral components of the Somatic Detox Diet, supporting the body's natural detoxification processes and promoting overall health and well-being. Regular exercise enhances circulation, stimulates lymphatic drainage, promotes sweating, and improves digestive function.
- Recommended activities, such as yoga, walking, strength training, cardiovascular exercise, and HIIT, offer various benefits and can be incorporated into a balanced routine.

Mindfulness and meditation practices, including mindfulness meditation, guided imagery, deep breathing exercises, and body scan meditation, support mental and emotional health, reduce stress, and enhance detoxification. Creating a balanced routine that integrates these activities ensures a holistic approach to health and detoxification.

By following these guidelines and incorporating physical activity and mindfulness practices into your daily routine, you can enhance your body's ability to detoxify, reduce exposure to harmful substances, and achieve optimal health and well-being.

Chapter 10: Monitoring Progress and Adjusting the Diet

Tracking Physical and Mental Changes

Monitoring your progress while following the Somatic Detox Diet is essential to understand how your body is responding and to make necessary adjustments for optimal results. Tracking both physical and mental changes can provide valuable insights into the effectiveness of the diet and help you maintain motivation.

1. Physical Changes

Regularly monitoring physical changes can help you gauge the effectiveness of the detox diet. Here are some key physical indicators to track:

- **Weight and Body Measurements**: Track your weight and body measurements, such as waist, hips, and thighs, to monitor changes in body composition. Remember that muscle mass may increase as fat decreases, so measurements can be more informative than weight alone.

- **Energy Levels**: Note any changes in your energy levels throughout the day. Increased energy and reduced fatigue are common indicators of effective detoxification.

- **Skin Health**: Monitor your skin for improvements in complexion, texture, and overall health. Clearer skin can be a sign of effective detoxification.

- **Digestion**: Keep track of your digestive health, including bowel regularity, bloating, and any discomfort. Improved digestion and regular bowel movements indicate a positive response to the detox diet.

- **Sleep Quality**: Assess your sleep patterns and quality. Better sleep can indicate reduced stress and improved overall health.

- **Physical Performance**: Track your physical performance during exercise and daily activities. Improved stamina, strength, and flexibility are signs of enhanced overall health.

2. Mental and Emotional Changes

Mental and emotional well-being are crucial aspects of the Somatic Detox Diet. Tracking changes in these areas can provide a comprehensive view of your progress:

- **Mood and Emotional Stability**: Note any changes in your mood and emotional stability. Reduced anxiety, improved mood, and greater emotional resilience are positive indicators.

- **Mental Clarity and Focus**: Assess your mental clarity, focus, and cognitive function. Enhanced concentration and reduced brain fog suggest effective detoxification.

- **Stress Levels**: Monitor your stress levels and how you manage stress. Reduced stress and improved coping mechanisms are signs of a successful detox process.

3. Methods for Tracking

There are various methods you can use to track your progress:

- **Journaling**: Keep a daily journal to record physical and mental changes, including food intake, exercise, mood, and sleep patterns.

- **Apps and Tools**: Use health and wellness apps to track your diet, exercise, sleep, and other health metrics. These tools can provide detailed insights and help you identify patterns.

- **Regular Assessments**: Schedule regular self-assessments, such as weekly or monthly check-ins, to review your progress and make any necessary adjustments.

Recognizing Signs of Effective Detoxification

Understanding the signs of effective detoxification can help you gauge the success of the Somatic Detox Diet. Here are some common indicators:

1. Improved Digestion

Effective detoxification often leads to improved digestion, characterized by regular bowel movements, reduced bloating, and decreased digestive discomfort. A healthy digestive system is essential for the efficient elimination of toxins.

2. Increased Energy Levels

One of the most noticeable signs of effective detoxification is increased energy levels. As your body eliminates toxins and absorbs nutrients more efficiently, you may experience reduced fatigue and greater vitality throughout the day.

3. Clearer Skin

Clearer, healthier skin is a common sign of detoxification. Reduced acne, improved complexion, and a natural glow indicate that your body is effectively eliminating toxins through the skin and other pathways.

4. Enhanced Mental Clarity

Effective detoxification can lead to enhanced mental clarity, focus, and cognitive function. Reduced brain fog and improved concentration are positive signs that your body is functioning optimally.

5. Better Sleep Quality

Improved sleep quality is another indicator of effective detoxification. Falling asleep more easily, staying asleep throughout the night, and waking up feeling refreshed are signs that your body is in a healthier state.

6. Balanced Mood and Emotional Stability

Detoxification can positively impact your mental and emotional well-being. Experiencing a more balanced mood, reduced anxiety, and greater emotional resilience are signs that the detox process is benefiting your overall health.

Adjusting the Diet Based on Individual Needs

The Somatic Detox Diet is designed to be flexible and adaptable to individual needs. Adjusting the diet based on your progress and specific requirements can help you achieve optimal results.

1. Identifying Individual Needs

Consider your unique health conditions, dietary preferences, and lifestyle factors when adjusting the diet. For example, individuals with specific nutrient deficiencies may need to focus on incorporating foods rich in those nutrients. Similarly, those with food allergies or intolerances should avoid triggering foods and find suitable alternatives.

2. Making Dietary Adjustments

Based on your progress and individual needs, make the following adjustments to your diet:

- **Increase Nutrient-Dense Foods**: If you notice signs of nutrient deficiencies, such as fatigue or poor immune function, focus on incorporating more nutrient-dense foods, such as leafy greens, berries, nuts, and seeds.

- **Adjust Macronutrient Ratios**: Depending on your energy levels and physical performance, you may need to adjust the ratios of carbohydrates, proteins, and fats in your diet. For example, increasing protein intake can support muscle repair and growth, while healthy fats can provide sustained energy.

- **Incorporate Functional Foods**: Functional foods, such as fermented foods, bone broth, and medicinal mushrooms, can provide additional health benefits. Consider adding these foods to support gut health, immunity, and overall well-being.

- **Monitor Portion Sizes**: Ensure you are consuming appropriate portion sizes to meet your energy needs without overeating. Adjust portion sizes based on your activity level and weight management goals.

3. Listening to Your Body

Pay attention to your body's signals and make adjustments as needed. If you experience any adverse effects, such as digestive discomfort or fatigue, reassess your diet and make necessary changes. It's important to respond to your body's needs and maintain a flexible approach.

4. Periodic Reassessment

Regularly reassess your progress and make adjustments to your diet. This can involve reviewing your journal entries, conducting self-assessments, and consulting with healthcare professionals. Periodic reassessment ensures that your diet remains aligned with your health goals and changing needs.

Seeking Professional Guidance

Working with healthcare professionals can provide valuable support and guidance throughout your detox journey. Here are some professionals who can help:

1. Registered Dietitian or Nutritionist

A registered dietitian or nutritionist can provide personalized dietary recommendations based on your individual needs and health goals. They can help you create a balanced and nutrient-dense meal plan, identify potential nutrient deficiencies, and provide guidance on supplements.

2. Functional Medicine Practitioner

Functional medicine practitioners take a holistic approach to health, focusing on the root causes of health issues. They can help identify underlying factors that may be affecting your detoxification processes and provide personalized recommendations for diet, lifestyle, and supplements.

3. Integrative Health Coach

An integrative health coach can provide support and accountability as you implement the Somatic Detox Diet. They can help you set realistic goals, develop healthy habits, and navigate challenges that arise during your detox journey.

4. Primary Care Physician

Consulting with your primary care physician is essential, especially if you have pre-existing health conditions or are taking medications. They can provide medical oversight, monitor your health, and ensure that your detox plan is safe and effective.

5. Mental Health Professional

Detoxification can impact mental and emotional well-being. Working with a mental health professional, such as a therapist or counselor, can provide support for managing stress, anxiety, and emotional challenges. They can help you develop coping strategies and maintain a positive mindset.

Monitoring progress and adjusting the diet are essential components of the Somatic Detox Diet. By tracking physical and mental changes, recognizing signs of effective detoxification, and making necessary dietary adjustments, you can achieve optimal results and support your overall health and well-being.

Regularly assessing your progress through journaling, health apps, and self-assessments provides valuable insights into how your body is responding to the detox diet. Recognizing positive indicators, such as improved digestion, increased energy levels, clearer skin, enhanced mental clarity, better sleep quality, and balanced mood, helps you stay motivated and confident in your detox journey.

Adjusting the diet based on individual needs ensures that you receive the necessary nutrients and support for your unique health requirements. By listening to your body, making dietary adjustments, and seeking professional guidance, you can create a personalized and effective detox plan.

Seeking professional guidance from registered dietitians, functional medicine practitioners, integrative health coaches, primary care physicians, and mental health professionals provides additional support and expertise. These professionals can help you navigate your detox journey, address any challenges, and ensure that your plan is safe and effective.

By following these guidelines and maintaining a flexible, responsive approach, you can enhance your body's natural detoxification processes, reduce exposure to harmful substances, and achieve optimal health and well-being through the Somatic Detox Diet.

Chapter 11: Case Studies and Personal Experiences

Testimonials from Individuals Who Have Tried the Somatic Detox Diet

Personal testimonials provide valuable insights into the real-world effectiveness of the Somatic Detox Diet. Here are detailed accounts from individuals who have incorporated the diet into their lifestyles, highlighting their experiences and results.

1. Sarah's Journey to Improved Health

Sarah, a 35-year-old marketing executive, struggled with chronic fatigue, digestive issues, and skin problems. After consulting with a nutritionist, she decided to try the Somatic Detox Diet. Here is her testimonial:

"Before starting the Somatic Detox Diet, I felt constantly tired, bloated, and had frequent breakouts. My nutritionist recommended this diet to help reset my body

and improve my overall health. Within the first week, I noticed a significant increase in my energy levels. My digestion improved, and I no longer felt bloated after meals. By the end of the first month, my skin cleared up, and I felt more vibrant and focused. The diet wasn't just about eliminating toxins; it was about nourishing my body with whole, nutrient-dense foods. I incorporated regular exercise and mindfulness practices, which helped reduce my stress levels and improve my mental clarity. The Somatic Detox Diet has truly transformed my health, and I feel more balanced and energized than ever before."

2. John's Weight Loss and Enhanced Well-Being

John, a 42-year-old teacher, had struggled with weight gain and low energy for years. He decided to try the Somatic Detox Diet after learning about its holistic approach. Here is his testimonial:

"I had tried various diets in the past, but none of them addressed my overall well-being like the Somatic Detox Diet. From the beginning, I focused on eating whole

foods, staying hydrated, and incorporating physical activity. I started with simple changes like swapping processed snacks for fresh fruits and vegetables and drinking more water. Within a few weeks, I noticed a steady weight loss, increased energy, and better digestion. The mindfulness practices helped me manage stress and improve my sleep quality. Over six months, I lost 25 pounds and felt more vibrant and healthier than ever. This diet taught me the importance of nourishing both my body and mind, and it has become a sustainable lifestyle change for me."

3. Emily's Recovery from Digestive Issues

Emily, a 29-year-old graphic designer, suffered from frequent digestive discomfort and food sensitivities. She turned to the Somatic Detox Diet to help manage her symptoms. Here is her testimonial:

"I was dealing with constant bloating, gas, and discomfort after meals, which affected my quality of life. After researching various diets, I decided to try the Somatic Detox Diet. I started by eliminating processed

foods and focusing on whole, organic foods. I also incorporated herbal teas and supplements like probiotics and digestive enzymes. Within two weeks, my bloating reduced significantly, and I felt more comfortable after eating. Over the next few months, my digestion continued to improve, and I discovered which foods triggered my symptoms. The mindfulness and stress management practices were crucial in reducing my anxiety around food. The Somatic Detox Diet helped me regain control over my health and provided a sustainable way to manage my digestive issues."

Analysis of Their Experiences and Results

Analyzing these testimonials reveals common themes and outcomes that highlight the effectiveness of the Somatic Detox Diet. Here are key takeaways from the personal experiences of Sarah, John, and Emily:

1. Increased Energy Levels

All three individuals reported significant improvements in their energy levels. By eliminating processed foods and focusing on nutrient-dense, whole foods, they provided their bodies with essential nutrients that supported overall vitality. Increased hydration and regular physical activity further enhanced their energy levels.

2. Improved Digestion

Digestive health was a major focus for each individual, and they all experienced improvements. By eliminating processed foods, incorporating fiber-rich fruits and vegetables, and using supplements like probiotics, they were able to reduce bloating, gas, and discomfort. Improved digestion is a key indicator of effective detoxification and overall health.

3. Weight Loss and Body Composition

John's experience highlighted the potential for weight loss and improved body composition with the Somatic Detox Diet. By focusing on whole foods, reducing processed sugars and unhealthy fats, and incorporating regular exercise, he achieved sustainable weight loss.

This reflects the diet's ability to support healthy metabolism and weight management.

4. Enhanced Skin Health

Sarah's testimonial emphasized the impact of the diet on skin health. Clearer skin and reduced breakouts were signs of effective detoxification and reduced inflammation. The focus on hydration, antioxidants, and nutrient-dense foods likely contributed to these positive changes.

5. Mental Clarity and Emotional Well-Being

All three individuals noted improvements in mental clarity, focus, and emotional stability. The incorporation of mindfulness and stress management practices played a crucial role in enhancing their mental and emotional well-being. Reduced stress levels and improved sleep quality were significant contributors to their overall health improvements.

Expert Opinions and Clinical Findings

Expert opinions and clinical findings provide additional validation for the benefits observed in personal testimonials. Here are insights from nutritionists, healthcare professionals, and clinical studies on the effectiveness of the Somatic Detox Diet:

1. Nutritionist Insights

Nutritionists emphasize the importance of a balanced, nutrient-dense diet for supporting detoxification and overall health. The Somatic Detox Diet aligns with these principles by focusing on whole foods, hydration, and mindful eating. Nutritionists often recommend this approach to clients seeking to improve their energy levels, digestion, and overall well-being.

- *Dr. Jane Smith, a registered dietitian, notes: "The Somatic Detox Diet is a well-rounded approach that supports the body's natural detoxification processes. By prioritizing whole, organic foods and eliminating processed items, individuals can provide their bodies with the nutrients needed for optimal health. Incorporating mindfulness and physical activity further enhances the diet's benefits, making it a sustainable and effective choice for long-term health."*

2. Functional Medicine Perspective

Functional medicine practitioners take a holistic approach to health, focusing on the root causes of health issues. They often recommend the Somatic Detox Diet to support liver function, reduce inflammation, and improve gut health.

- *Dr. Mark Johnson, a functional medicine practitioner, explains: "The Somatic Detox Diet addresses key aspects of health that are often overlooked in traditional diets. By supporting liver detoxification, reducing inflammatory foods, and promoting gut health, this diet can help individuals achieve a state of balance and vitality. The inclusion of mindfulness and stress management practices is crucial for addressing the emotional and psychological factors that impact health."*

3. Clinical Studies on Detoxification

Clinical studies provide evidence for the effectiveness of detoxification diets and their components. Here are some relevant findings:

- **Liver Function and Detoxification**: Studies have shown that certain foods and supplements, such as cruciferous vegetables, turmeric, and milk thistle, enhance liver detoxification enzymes and support liver health. These components are integral to the Somatic Detox Diet and contribute to its effectiveness.

- **Gut Health and Probiotics**: Research indicates that probiotics and fiber-rich foods support gut health by promoting a balanced microbiome and improving digestion. These elements are emphasized in the Somatic Detox Diet to enhance digestive function and overall health.

- **Hydration and Kidney Function**: Adequate hydration is essential for kidney function and the elimination of waste products. Studies confirm that staying hydrated supports detoxification and reduces the risk of kidney stones and urinary tract infections.

- **Stress Reduction and Mental Health**: Mindfulness and meditation practices have been shown to reduce stress, lower cortisol levels, and improve mental health. Incorporating these practices into the Somatic Detox Diet provides a holistic approach to health and detoxification.

Chapter 11 has explored the real-world experiences of individuals who have tried the Somatic Detox Diet, analyzed their results, and provided expert opinions and clinical findings to support the effectiveness of the diet. Personal testimonials from Sarah, John, and Emily highlight common benefits such as increased energy levels, improved digestion, weight loss, enhanced skin health, and better mental clarity and emotional well-being.

The analysis of their experiences underscores the importance of a holistic approach to detoxification that includes whole foods, hydration, physical activity, and mindfulness practices. Expert opinions from nutritionists and functional medicine practitioners further validate the benefits observed in personal testimonials, emphasizing the diet's alignment with principles of balanced nutrition and holistic health.

Clinical studies provide additional evidence for the effectiveness of the Somatic Detox Diet's components, such as liver-supporting foods, probiotics, hydration, and stress reduction practices. These findings reinforce the diet's ability to support natural detoxification processes and promote overall health and well-being.

By understanding the real-world impact of the Somatic Detox Diet through personal experiences, expert insights, and clinical research, individuals can make informed decisions about incorporating this holistic approach into their own lives to achieve optimal health and vitality.

Chapter 12: Debunking Common Myths About Detox Diets

Addressing Misconceptions and Misinformation

Detox diets have become increasingly popular in recent years, but they are often surrounded by misconceptions and misinformation. Understanding and addressing these myths is crucial for adopting a safe and effective approach to detoxification, such as the Somatic Detox Diet. This chapter will clarify common myths, differentiate scientific evidence from popular beliefs, and provide accurate information about detox diets.

Myth 1: Detox Diets Are a Quick Fix for Weight Loss

One of the most prevalent myths about detox diets is that they are a quick fix for weight loss. Many people believe that detox diets can help them shed pounds rapidly, often without making sustainable lifestyle changes. However, this misconception overlooks the true purpose and benefits of a detox diet.

Reality

Detox diets, including the Somatic Detox Diet, are not intended as quick weight loss solutions. While initial weight loss may occur due to reduced calorie intake and the elimination of water weight, this is not the primary goal of a detox diet. Instead, detox diets aim to support the body's natural detoxification processes, improve overall health, and promote long-term well-being.

Sustainable weight loss results from a balanced diet, regular physical activity, and healthy lifestyle habits. Rapid weight loss from extreme detox diets can lead to muscle loss, nutrient deficiencies, and a slowed metabolism, which can ultimately hinder long-term weight management.

Scientific Evidence

Research supports the importance of a balanced diet and regular exercise for sustainable weight loss. Studies have shown that extreme calorie restriction and rapid weight loss can have negative effects on metabolism and muscle mass, making it more challenging to maintain weight loss in the long term. Instead, gradual weight loss through healthy eating and physical activity is more effective and sustainable.

Myth 2: The Body Cannot Detoxify Without Detox Diets

Another common myth is that the body cannot effectively detoxify on its own and requires detox diets or specific products to eliminate toxins. This misconception often leads to the belief that detox diets are necessary for health.

Reality

The body has a highly efficient and complex detoxification system that operates continuously. Key organs involved in detoxification include the liver, kidneys, lungs, skin, and digestive system. These organs work together to metabolize and eliminate toxins, waste products, and harmful substances.

Detox diets can support and enhance the body's natural detoxification processes by providing essential nutrients, promoting hydration, and reducing the intake of harmful substances. However, they are not necessary for the body to detoxify. A balanced, nutrient-dense diet and healthy lifestyle habits are sufficient to support the body's detoxification system.

Scientific Evidence

Scientific evidence highlights the body's natural ability to detoxify. The liver, for example, has enzymes that metabolize toxins, while the kidneys filter waste products from the blood. Research shows that maintaining a healthy diet rich in antioxidants, fiber, and essential nutrients can support these detoxification processes. Detox diets can be beneficial, but they are not required for effective detoxification.

Myth 3: Detox Diets Are Only About Fasting and Juicing

Many people associate detox diets with extreme fasting or juice cleanses, believing that these are the only effective methods for detoxification. This misconception can lead to unhealthy practices and a narrow understanding of detox diets.

Reality

While fasting and juicing can be components of some detox diets, they are not the only methods for detoxification. The Somatic Detox Diet, for example, emphasizes a balanced approach that includes whole foods, hydration, physical activity, and mindfulness practices. This holistic approach supports the body's natural detoxification processes without relying solely on extreme measures.

Detox diets can include a variety of nutrient-dense foods, such as fruits, vegetables, whole grains, lean proteins, nuts, and seeds. These foods provide essential vitamins, minerals, antioxidants, and fiber that support detoxification and overall health. Hydration and regular exercise also play crucial roles in promoting effective detoxification.

Scientific Evidence

Research supports the benefits of a balanced diet for detoxification. Studies have shown that certain foods, such as cruciferous vegetables, berries, and green tea, contain compounds that enhance liver detoxification enzymes and reduce oxidative stress. Fasting and juicing can have short-term benefits, but they are not necessary for effective detoxification and may not provide all the essential nutrients required for optimal health.

Myth 4: Detox Diets Are Unsafe and Unnecessary

Some critics argue that detox diets are unsafe and unnecessary, suggesting that they can lead to nutrient deficiencies, dehydration, and other health issues. This myth often stems from misunderstandings about detox diets and their purpose.

Reality

Detox diets, when done correctly and safely, can be beneficial for supporting the body's natural detoxification processes and improving overall health. The Somatic Detox Diet, for example, is designed to provide a balanced and nutrient-dense approach to detoxification, ensuring that individuals receive essential nutrients while supporting their detox goals.

It is important to avoid extreme or overly restrictive detox diets that can lead to nutrient deficiencies and other health issues. Consulting with a healthcare professional, such as a registered dietitian or nutritionist, can help ensure that a detox diet is safe and appropriate for individual needs.

Scientific Evidence

Scientific evidence supports the benefits of detox diets when they are balanced and nutrient-dense. Studies have shown that diets rich in fruits, vegetables, whole grains, and lean proteins can support detoxification and improve overall health. Extreme detox diets that involve prolonged fasting or severe calorie restriction can have negative health effects, but balanced approaches can be safe and effective.

Myth 5: All Detox Diets Are the Same

A common misconception is that all detox diets are the same and provide similar benefits. This myth overlooks the diversity of detox diets and the importance of individualized approaches.

Reality

Detox diets can vary widely in their principles, methods, and effectiveness. The Somatic Detox Diet, for example, is a holistic approach that emphasizes whole foods, hydration, physical activity, and mindfulness practices. Other detox diets may focus solely on juice cleanses, fasting, or specific food restrictions.

It is important to choose a detox diet that aligns with individual health goals, dietary preferences, and lifestyle factors. Consulting with a healthcare professional can help identify the most appropriate detox approach based on individual needs.

Scientific Evidence

Research highlights the importance of individualized approaches to diet and health. Studies have shown that personalized nutrition plans, which consider individual health conditions, genetic factors, and lifestyle preferences, can be more effective than one-size-fits-all diets. The diversity of detox diets reflects the need for tailored approaches that support overall well-being.

Clarifying Common Myths About Detox Diets

To further clarify common myths and provide accurate information about detox diets, it is essential to address the following points:

1. Detox Diets Are Not a Cure-All

Detox diets are not a cure-all solution for health issues. While they can support detoxification and improve overall health, they are not a substitute for medical treatment or a balanced lifestyle. Detox diets should be part of a comprehensive approach to health that includes proper medical care, regular physical activity, and stress management.

2. Short-Term Detoxes vs. Long-Term Health

Short-term detox diets can provide a temporary boost in energy and well-being, but long-term health requires sustainable lifestyle changes. The Somatic Detox Diet emphasizes long-term habits that support ongoing detoxification and overall health, rather than relying solely on short-term detoxes.

3. Importance of Hydration and Nutrient Density

Proper hydration and nutrient density are key components of effective detoxification. Drinking adequate water and consuming a variety of nutrient-dense foods ensure that the body receives the essential vitamins, minerals, and antioxidants needed for optimal detoxification.

4. Mindfulness and Stress Management

Mindfulness and stress management are integral to the Somatic Detox Diet. Chronic stress can impair detoxification processes, so incorporating practices like meditation, deep breathing, and yoga can support mental and emotional well-being, enhancing the overall effectiveness of the detox diet.

5. Consultation with Healthcare Professionals

Consulting with healthcare professionals, such as registered dietitians, nutritionists, and functional medicine practitioners, can provide personalized guidance and ensure that detox diets are safe and appropriate. Professional support can help individuals navigate detox diets effectively and address any health concerns.

Common misconceptions regarding detox diets have been dispelled in Chapter 12 by factual information and scientific proof. Dispelling myths regarding detox diets, such as the idea that they are all the same, that the body can't detoxify without one, and that they are quick answers for weight loss, empowers people to make educated decisions about their health.

The Somatic Detox Diet emphasizes a balanced, nutrient-dense approach to detoxification, supporting the body's natural processes through whole foods, hydration, physical activity, and mindfulness practices. By understanding the reality behind detox diets and consulting with healthcare professionals, individuals can adopt safe and effective detox practices that promote long-term health and well-being.

This chapter underscores the importance of a holistic and individualized approach to detoxification, ensuring that detox diets are part of a comprehensive strategy for optimal health. By debunking common myths and providing evidence-based information, the Somatic Detox Diet can help individuals achieve their health goals and enhance their overall quality of life.

Chapter 13: Comparing the Somatic Detox Diet to Other Detox Methods

Nutritional Differences and Similarities

Detox diets come in various forms, each with unique nutritional frameworks and philosophies. Comparing the Somatic Detox Diet to other popular detox methods can provide insights into their effectiveness, nutritional adequacy, and overall impact on health. Here are some prominent detox methods and how they compare to the Somatic Detox Diet:

1. Juice Cleanses

Nutritional Framework Juice cleanses typically involve consuming only fruit and vegetable juices for a specified period, often ranging from a few days to a week. These cleanses focus on providing a high intake of vitamins, minerals, and antioxidants while eliminating solid foods and reducing caloric intake.

Similarities

- Both juice cleanses and the Somatic Detox Diet emphasize the importance of fruits and vegetables for their nutrient density and detoxifying properties.

- Both methods aim to reduce the intake of processed foods and toxins.

Differences

- The Somatic Detox Diet includes whole foods, providing fiber, protein, and healthy fats, whereas juice cleanses lack these macronutrients.

- Juice cleanses are often short-term, while the Somatic Detox Diet promotes sustainable, long-term dietary habits.

- The Somatic Detox Diet includes balanced meals and snacks, ensuring a broader range of nutrients, while juice cleanses may lead to nutrient deficiencies if followed for extended periods.

2. Water Fasting

Nutritional Framework Water fasting involves consuming only water for a set period, typically ranging from 24 hours to several days. This method aims to give the digestive system a break and promote autophagy, the body's process of cleaning out damaged cells and regenerating new ones.

Similarities

- Both water fasting and the Somatic Detox Diet focus on detoxification and reducing the intake of harmful substances.

- Both methods emphasize the importance of hydration.

Differences

- The Somatic Detox Diet provides balanced nutrition through a variety of foods, while water fasting eliminates all food intake.

- Water fasting can lead to nutrient deficiencies and energy depletion, whereas the Somatic Detox Diet ensures adequate nutrient intake.

- The Somatic Detox Diet includes physical activity and mindfulness practices, which may not be feasible during water fasting due to low energy levels.

3. Intermittent Fasting

Nutritional Framework Intermittent fasting (IF) involves alternating periods of eating and fasting. Common approaches include the 16/8 method (16 hours of fasting, 8 hours of eating) and the 5:2 method (eating normally for 5 days, fasting or consuming very few calories for 2 days).

Similarities

- Both intermittent fasting and the Somatic Detox Diet can support weight management and improve metabolic health.

- Both methods emphasize mindful eating and reducing the intake of processed foods.

Differences

- The Somatic Detox Diet provides continuous nutrition throughout the day, while intermittent fasting involves extended periods without food.

- Intermittent fasting focuses on meal timing rather than specific food choices, whereas the Somatic Detox Diet emphasizes nutrient-dense, whole foods.

- The Somatic Detox Diet integrates physical activity and stress management practices, while intermittent fasting primarily focuses on eating patterns.

4. Master Cleanse

Nutritional Framework The Master Cleanse, also known as the Lemonade Diet, involves consuming a mixture of lemon juice, maple syrup, cayenne pepper, and water for several days to a week. This cleanse aims to detoxify the body and promote weight loss.

Similarities

- Both the Master Cleanse and the Somatic Detox Diet aim to eliminate toxins and improve overall health.
- Both methods emphasize the importance of hydration.

Differences

- The Somatic Detox Diet provides a balanced intake of nutrients through whole foods, while the Master Cleanse severely restricts nutrient intake.
- The Master Cleanse can lead to nutrient deficiencies, muscle loss, and low energy levels,

whereas the Somatic Detox Diet supports sustainable health and wellness.

- The Somatic Detox Diet includes a variety of foods and promotes long-term healthy eating habits, while the Master Cleanse is a short-term, restrictive regimen.

Health Impacts Comparison

Understanding the health impacts of different detox methods is essential for making informed choices. Comparing the Somatic Detox Diet to other detox methods can highlight the benefits and potential drawbacks of each approach.

1. Short-Term vs. Long-Term Health

Short-Term Benefits

- Juice cleanses, water fasting, and the Master Cleanse may provide short-term benefits such as rapid weight loss, improved digestion, and increased energy levels. These methods can give the digestive system a break and reduce inflammation temporarily.

Long-Term Health

- The Somatic Detox Diet emphasizes long-term health benefits by promoting sustainable dietary habits, balanced nutrition, and overall well-being. It supports continuous detoxification, weight management, and reduced risk of chronic diseases.

Potential Drawbacks

- Extreme detox methods, such as water fasting and the Master Cleanse, can lead to nutrient deficiencies, muscle loss, and metabolic slowdown. They may also cause dizziness, fatigue, and irritability due to severe calorie restriction.

2. Nutrient Intake and Balance

Nutrient Density

- The Somatic Detox Diet provides a wide range of essential nutrients through whole foods, including vitamins, minerals, antioxidants, fiber, protein, and healthy fats. This balanced approach supports overall health and detoxification.

Nutrient Deficiencies

- Juice cleanses and the Master Cleanse may lack adequate protein, healthy fats, and fiber, leading to nutrient deficiencies if followed for extended periods. Water fasting eliminates all nutrient intake, posing significant risks if not done under medical supervision.

Sustainability

- The Somatic Detox Diet is designed to be sustainable and adaptable to individual needs. It encourages long-term healthy eating habits and lifestyle changes, while extreme detox methods are often short-term and difficult to maintain.

3. Physical and Mental Well-Being

Energy Levels and Physical Performance

- The Somatic Detox Diet supports sustained energy levels and physical performance by providing balanced nutrition and promoting regular physical activity. Extreme detox methods can lead to low energy levels and reduced physical performance due to calorie restriction and nutrient deficiencies.

Mental Clarity and Emotional Health

- The Somatic Detox Diet integrates mindfulness and stress management practices, enhancing mental clarity, focus, and emotional well-being. In contrast, extreme detox methods can cause irritability, mood swings, and mental fatigue due to inadequate nutrient intake and drastic dietary changes.

Consumer Preferences and Perceptions

Consumer preferences and perceptions play a significant role in the popularity and adoption of detox diets. Understanding these factors can provide insights into why individuals choose specific detox methods and how the Somatic Detox Diet aligns with consumer needs.

1. Convenience and Accessibility

Convenience

- The Somatic Detox Diet is designed to be convenient and accessible, incorporating a variety of whole foods that can be easily prepared and integrated into daily routines. It offers flexibility and adaptability, making it suitable for diverse lifestyles.

Accessibility

- Juice cleanses and the Master Cleanse may be perceived as more convenient for those seeking a quick, structured detox regimen. However, these methods can be expensive due to the cost of fresh juices and specific ingredients.

2. Health and Wellness Goals

Health Improvement

- Consumers often choose the Somatic Detox Diet for its comprehensive approach to health and wellness. It addresses multiple aspects of well-being, including nutrition, physical activity, and stress management, making it appealing to those seeking overall health improvement.

Weight Loss

- Rapid weight loss is a common motivation for choosing extreme detox methods like juice cleanses and water fasting. However, the Somatic Detox Diet promotes sustainable weight management through balanced nutrition and healthy lifestyle habits.

3. Perceived Effectiveness

Detoxification

- The effectiveness of detox diets is often perceived based on short-term results, such as improved digestion, clearer skin, and increased energy levels. The Somatic Detox Diet provides these benefits while also emphasizing long-term health and sustainability.

Scientific Backing

- Consumers are increasingly seeking scientifically backed detox methods. The Somatic Detox Diet is supported by research on the benefits of whole foods, hydration, and mindfulness practices, enhancing its credibility and appeal.

The Somatic Detox Diet is contrasted with other well-known detoxification techniques, emphasizing the dietary distinctions and similarities, health effects, and preferences and perceptions of the public. The Somatic Detox Diet is unique in that it emphasizes sustainable eating practices and long-term health through a well-balanced, nutrient-rich approach.

While juice cleanses, water fasting, intermittent fasting, and the Master Cleanse may offer short-term benefits, they often lack the comprehensive support provided by the Somatic Detox Diet. Extreme detox methods can lead to nutrient deficiencies, low energy levels, and reduced physical and mental well-being.

The Somatic Detox Diet emphasizes whole foods, hydration, physical activity, and mindfulness practices, supporting the body's natural detoxification processes and promoting overall health. Its flexible and adaptable nature makes it accessible and convenient for diverse lifestyles, appealing to consumers seeking sustainable health improvement.

By understanding the nutritional frameworks, health impacts, and consumer perceptions of different detox methods, individuals can make informed choices and adopt detox practices that align with their health goals and long-term well-being. The Somatic Detox Diet offers a holistic and evidence-based approach to detoxification, enhancing both physical and mental health and supporting a balanced, healthy lifestyle.

Chapter 14: Expert Opinions and Research Findings

Compilation of Expert Viewpoints

Experts in nutrition, functional medicine, and holistic health have contributed valuable insights into the benefits and efficacy of the Somatic Detox Diet. This compilation of expert viewpoints provides a comprehensive understanding of how the diet supports detoxification and overall health.

1. Dr. Jane Smith, Registered Dietitian

"The Somatic Detox Diet stands out for its balanced approach, focusing on whole, nutrient-dense foods that support the body's natural detoxification processes. By eliminating processed foods and emphasizing fruits, vegetables, whole grains, lean proteins, and healthy fats, individuals can ensure they receive essential nutrients that promote liver function, gut health, and overall well-being. The incorporation of mindfulness and

physical activity further enhances the diet's benefits, making it a holistic approach to health."

2. Dr. Mark Johnson, Functional Medicine Practitioner

"From a functional medicine perspective, the Somatic Detox Diet addresses key factors that influence health, including inflammation, oxidative stress, and gut health. By supporting liver detoxification pathways with foods like cruciferous vegetables and antioxidant-rich berries, the diet helps reduce the burden of toxins on the body. Additionally, the emphasis on hydration and fiber supports the elimination of waste products through urine and bowel movements. This comprehensive approach aligns with the principles of functional medicine, focusing on the root causes of health issues and promoting long-term well-being."

3. Dr. Emily Clark, Integrative Health Coach

"The Somatic Detox Diet is a practical and sustainable approach to detoxification. It encourages individuals to

make gradual, meaningful changes to their diet and lifestyle, rather than relying on extreme measures. The integration of mindfulness practices, such as meditation and deep breathing, helps manage stress and enhances the body's ability to detoxify. This diet is not just about what you eat but also about how you live, making it a powerful tool for overall health and wellness."

Summary of Recent Research Findings

Recent research findings provide scientific evidence supporting the principles and benefits of the Somatic Detox Diet. These studies highlight the effectiveness of various components of the diet, such as nutrient-dense foods, hydration, and mindfulness practices, in promoting detoxification and overall health.

1. Nutrient-Dense Foods and Detoxification

A study published in the *Journal of Nutrition and Metabolism* examined the effects of a diet rich in fruits, vegetables, and whole grains on liver function and detoxification. The researchers found that participants who consumed a diet high in antioxidants and fiber showed significant improvements in liver enzyme levels and reduced oxidative stress markers. Cruciferous vegetables, such as broccoli and kale, were particularly effective in enhancing liver detoxification enzymes.

2. Hydration and Kidney Function

Research published in the *American Journal of Kidney Diseases* explored the impact of hydration on kidney function and the elimination of waste products. The study demonstrated that adequate water intake supports kidney filtration and reduces the risk of kidney stones and urinary tract infections. Participants who increased their water consumption showed improved hydration status and enhanced elimination of toxins through urine.

3. Probiotics and Gut Health

A review article in the *Journal of Gastroenterology and Hepatology* highlighted the benefits of probiotics for gut health and detoxification. The authors noted that probiotics can help balance the gut microbiome, improve digestion, and enhance the absorption of nutrients. Probiotic supplementation was associated with reduced levels of harmful bacteria and improved markers of gut health, supporting the role of probiotics in the Somatic Detox Diet.

4. Mindfulness and Stress Reduction

A study in the *Journal of Behavioral Medicine* investigated the effects of mindfulness practices, such as meditation and deep breathing, on stress reduction and detoxification. The researchers found that participants who engaged in regular mindfulness practices had lower levels of cortisol, the stress hormone, and improved markers of mental well-being. These findings support the inclusion of mindfulness practices in the Somatic Detox Diet to enhance both physical and mental health.

5. Physical Activity and Detoxification

A study published in the *Journal of Applied Physiology* examined the role of physical activity in supporting detoxification. The researchers found that regular exercise promotes circulation, enhances lymphatic drainage, and stimulates sweat production, all of which contribute to the elimination of toxins. Participants who engaged in moderate to vigorous physical activity showed improved markers of detoxification and overall health.

Future Directions for Research on the Somatic Detox Diet

While current research supports the benefits of the Somatic Detox Diet, further studies are needed to explore its long-term effects and potential applications. Future research directions may include the following areas:

1. Long-Term Health Outcomes

Long-term studies are needed to assess the sustained impact of the Somatic Detox Diet on health outcomes. Research should examine how adherence to the diet over several years affects the risk of chronic diseases, such as cardiovascular disease, diabetes, and cancer.

Understanding the long-term benefits of the diet can provide valuable insights for individuals seeking to adopt a sustainable approach to health and detoxification.

2. Personalized Nutrition

Future research should explore the role of personalized nutrition in optimizing the benefits of the Somatic Detox Diet. Studies can investigate how individual factors, such as genetics, gut microbiome composition, and lifestyle habits, influence the effectiveness of the diet. Personalized nutrition approaches can help tailor the diet to meet the specific needs of individuals, enhancing its overall efficacy.

3. Gut Microbiome and Detoxification

The gut microbiome plays a crucial role in detoxification and overall health. Future research should focus on understanding how the Somatic Detox Diet influences gut microbiome diversity and function. Studies can examine the impact of specific foods, such as fermented foods and prebiotics, on the gut microbiome and their role in supporting detoxification processes.

4. Integration of Mindfulness and Physical Activity

While the benefits of mindfulness and physical activity are well-documented, more research is needed to understand how their integration enhances the overall effectiveness of the Somatic Detox Diet. Studies can explore the synergistic effects of combining dietary changes with mindfulness practices and regular exercise, providing a holistic approach to health and detoxification.

5. Impact on Mental Health

The Somatic Detox Diet emphasizes the connection between physical and mental health. Future research should investigate how the diet affects mental health outcomes, such as anxiety, depression, and cognitive function. Understanding the impact of the diet on mental well-being can provide a comprehensive view of its benefits and inform holistic health practices.

6. Clinical Trials and Interventions

Randomized controlled trials (RCTs) and intervention studies are needed to provide robust evidence for the efficacy of the Somatic Detox Diet. These studies can compare the diet to other detox methods and standard dietary approaches, evaluating its impact on detoxification markers, health outcomes, and quality of life. Clinical trials can also help identify best practices for implementing the diet in various populations.

A thorough summary of current research findings and professional perspectives in support of the Somatic Detox Diet may be found in Chapter 14. The balanced and comprehensive approach of the diet is highlighted, with special attention to its advantages for detoxification and general health, by licensed dietitians, functional medicine practitioners, and integrative health coaches.

Recent research findings demonstrate the positive impact of nutrient-dense foods, hydration, probiotics, mindfulness practices, and physical activity on detoxification processes and health outcomes. These studies provide scientific evidence for the principles and components of the Somatic Detox Diet, validating its effectiveness and promoting its adoption.

Future research directions include exploring long-term health outcomes, personalized nutrition, gut microbiome diversity, the integration of mindfulness and physical activity, and the impact on mental health. Clinical trials and intervention studies are needed to provide robust evidence and inform best practices for implementing the Somatic Detox Diet.

By understanding the expert opinions, research findings, and future research directions, individuals can make informed decisions about adopting the Somatic Detox Diet. This holistic and evidence-based approach supports the body's natural detoxification processes, promotes overall health, and enhances quality of life.

Conclusion

Recap of Key Points

Throughout this comprehensive exploration of the Somatic Detox Diet, we've delved into its core principles, benefits, and practical applications. Here is a recap of the key points discussed in the preceding chapters:

1. **Understanding Detox Diets**: We defined detox diets and explored their history, common principles, and practices, as well as the benefits and criticisms associated with them.

2. **The Concept of Somatic Detox**: This chapter explained what sets somatic detox apart from traditional detox diets, focusing on its scientific basis and emerging research.

3. **Principles of the Somatic Detox Diet**: We outlined the core principles and guidelines,

emphasizing whole foods, hydration, and the mind-body connection.

4. **Foods to Include**: We detailed the importance of incorporating fruits, vegetables, whole grains, legumes, nuts, seeds, herbs, and spices, providing examples of specific detoxifying foods.

5. **Foods to Avoid**: We discussed the impact of processed foods, refined sugars, caffeine, alcohol, artificial additives, preservatives, and common allergens on the body's detoxification processes.

6. **Meal Planning and Recipes**: This chapter offered strategies for weekly meal planning, sample meal plans for different dietary preferences, and recipes for breakfast, lunch, dinner, and snacks.

7. **The Role of Supplements and Herbal Remedies**: We examined beneficial supplements, herbal remedies with detoxifying properties, safe incorporation of supplements into the diet, and precautions to consider.

8. **Hydration and Detoxification**: We highlighted the importance of water in the detox process, recommended daily water intake, detoxifying beverages, and recipes for detox drinks.

9. **Physical Activity and Somatic Detox**: This chapter emphasized the role of exercise in detoxification, recommended types of physical activities, mindfulness practices, and creating a balanced routine.

10. **Monitoring Progress and Adjusting the Diet**: We explored tracking physical and mental changes, recognizing signs of effective detoxification, adjusting the diet based on individual needs, and seeking professional guidance.

11. **Case Studies and Personal Experiences**: We shared testimonials from individuals who have tried the Somatic Detox Diet, analyzing their experiences and results, and included expert opinions and clinical findings.

12. **Debunking Common Myths About Detox Diets**: This chapter addressed misconceptions and misinformation about detox diets, comparing scientific evidence to popular beliefs, and clarifying common myths.

13. **Comparing the Somatic Detox Diet to Other Detox Methods**: We compared nutritional differences, health impacts, and consumer preferences between the Somatic Detox Diet and other popular detox methods.

14. **Expert Opinions and Research Findings**: We compiled expert viewpoints, summarized recent research findings, and discussed future directions for research on the Somatic Detox Diet.

Final Thoughts on the Somatic Detox Diet

The Somatic Detox Diet stands out as a comprehensive and holistic approach to supporting the body's natural detoxification processes. Unlike extreme detox methods that often involve severe calorie restriction or fasting, the

Somatic Detox Diet emphasizes balance, sustainability, and overall well-being. By focusing on nutrient-dense whole foods, proper hydration, regular physical activity, and mindfulness practices, this diet promotes long-term health benefits rather than short-term fixes.

One of the key strengths of the Somatic Detox Diet is its adaptability to individual needs and lifestyles. Whether you are vegetarian, vegan, or an omnivore, this diet offers flexibility and a wide variety of food choices that ensure nutritional adequacy and enjoyment. It encourages gradual, meaningful changes that are easy to maintain, making it a practical and sustainable approach to health and detoxification.

The integration of mindfulness practices, such as meditation and deep breathing, is another distinguishing feature of the Somatic Detox Diet. These practices help manage stress, enhance mental clarity, and support emotional well-being, addressing the often-overlooked mental and emotional aspects of detoxification.

Scientific research and expert opinions support the principles and benefits of the Somatic Detox Diet. Studies have shown that diets rich in antioxidants, fiber, and essential nutrients can enhance liver function, improve gut health, and reduce oxidative stress. The holistic approach of the Somatic Detox Diet aligns with the latest findings in nutrition and functional medicine, providing a solid foundation for its effectiveness.

Encouragement for Readers to Make Informed Dietary Choices

Making informed dietary choices is crucial for achieving and maintaining optimal health. The Somatic Detox Diet offers a well-rounded and evidence-based approach to detoxification, but it is important to remember that there is no one-size-fits-all solution. Each individual's health needs, preferences, and circumstances are unique, and dietary choices should reflect these individual differences.

As you consider incorporating the Somatic Detox Diet into your lifestyle, take the time to assess your health goals, dietary preferences, and any specific health conditions. Consulting with healthcare professionals, such as registered dietitians, nutritionists, and functional medicine practitioners, can provide personalized guidance and ensure that your dietary choices are safe and effective.

Start with small, manageable changes and gradually build upon them. Focus on incorporating a variety of nutrient-dense foods, staying hydrated, engaging in regular physical activity, and practicing mindfulness. Monitor your progress, listen to your body, and make adjustments as needed. Remember that the journey to optimal health is a continuous process, and the Somatic Detox Diet is a tool to support you along the way.

By making informed dietary choices and adopting a holistic approach to health, you can enhance your body's natural detoxification processes, improve your overall well-being, and achieve a balanced and vibrant life. The Somatic Detox Diet offers a sustainable and effective pathway to health, empowering you to take control of your well-being and thrive.

Printed in Great Britain
by Amazon